PRAISE FOR *RAG DOLLS AND RAGE*

While it is a truism that we are all broken vessels, some of us are more seaworthy than others. Incredibly, some manage to stay afloat despite massive gashes hidden deep below the surface. Sheila Tucker is one such person. In her compelling memoir *n   d Rage*, she delves into her perplexing pas*   ders into her most private experienc   arrative replete with family secrets, l   detritus of trauma. A tale of resilienc   Tucker is ultimately able to discard   childhood and approach the shore of a saf   _, a long, arduous journey.

Christine Arthurs
Director of the Literary Section, The Toronto Heliconian Club

A mystery and fiction reviewer usually reads an autobiography for one primary reason—there's a great story that grabs hold of you and doesn't let go. It is a focused personal journey in a book. And successfully telling the tale in the first person adds to the challenge and rewards. Strong, autobiographical storytelling is rare, and *Rag Dolls and Rage* is a poignant and passionate example of telling a life story you can't put down. It's a voyage, a circus, and a vicious circle that sparkles with insight and guidance cast alongside moments of delight, anguish and abuse. You are surrounded by the fortitude of a person who survived and thrived in her life and now presents it in a story. *Rag Dolls and Rage* by Sheila Tucker is a journey to be experienced.

Don Graves, *The Bay Observer*

Rag Dolls and Rage is a raw and honest account of the emotional bruises we endure as children, invisible but potent, weighty and suffocating, and how they cling to us and shape our sense of self. But mostly, it's a powerful story of survival, reconciliation and hope. Sheila Tucker has laid bare her pain and haunted past, but graciously allows us to follow her on her journey of healing. The result is a tribute to the indomitable human spirit.

Cindy Watson, Founder, Women on Purpose
President, Muskoka Authors Association President

Rag Dolls and Rage is a beautifully written and compelling personal story of a childhood sexual assault survivor's resiliency and strength. This heartfelt piece stands as a true testament to the perseverance of survivors. The reader moves through the fear, lack of trust and identity crises that survivors of sexual assault often navigate alone. The path to healing and reclaiming one's agency and voice can be a long one, yet Sheila shows that it is possible. This book is powerful. Thank you for sharing your story, Sheila.

Alma Arguello, Executive Director,
SAVIS (Sexual Assault and Violence Intervention Services) of Halton

Sheila Tucker has written a spellbinding account of growing up in a dysfunctional environment. It's a captivating read from beginning to end. How she survived and remained somewhat "normal" is a testimony to her drive and determination to escape and become who the higher power has blessed her to be. This is a story that is sure to help and encourage those who struggle with internal issues of abuse, rejection and abandonment.

Reverend Minister Dennis Curley, ThM.
Student, Toronto Centre for Psychotherapy and Counselling Education

Opening a cardboard box of family memorabilia forgotten in the basement, the protagonist of this gripping autobiography is overcome with raw childhood pain. Seeking closure, she begins telling her life story to Dr. Beal, a psychologist: each session a riveting chapter intended to "break up a jigsaw of cuts and bruises." Transported back in time, Sheila relives both the joys and traumas of her formative years in '60s Britain. Dr. Beal helps her reframe her sense of self and, finally, exorcise her demons. In this riveting retelling, Sheila finds redemption and offers hope to others with the inspiring message that it is possible to break free from a painful past.

Josie Di Sciascio-Andrews, author, *How the Italians Created Canada*, *A Jar of Fireflies* and *In the Name of Hockey*

RAG DOLLS AND RAGE

Sheila E. Tucker

ISBN: 978-1-9991073-0-7 (print)
ISBN: 978-1-9991073-1-4 (electronic)

Cover Photos: from family collection
Cover Stock Art: Fresh Soul Photography/Shutterstock.com

For information: ragdollsandrage.com

First edition
Published and printed in Canada

The following story is based upon true events. For the purposes of privacy and discretion, some names and locations have been changed. Information provided herein reflects solely the author's viewpoint. Any resemblance to actual persons, living or dead, business establishments, events, or locales is entirely coincidental or based on the author's perspective.

The content of this book does not constitute advice and should not be construed as such. Readers must consult appropriate professionals for information relevant to their specific situation, particularly before starting, changing or discontinuing anything.

Please note that this memoir contains mature content, sexuality, violence and coarse language.

Library and Archives Canada registration, cover design and production management through the TRI Publishing™ program TRIMATRIX Management Consulting Inc. (www.trimatrixmanagement.com). This book was written, edited and published by the author/publisher. TRIMATRIX Management Consulting Inc. assumes no responsibility for damages, direct or indirect, from publication of the included works. Work is included as provided by the author/publisher, views expressed are those of the author/publisher and any errors, omissions or otherwise are the author's/publisher's responsibility.

Author's Note

I have people to thank for helping make this book possible.

Early readers were Marj Cripps, Pat Parkinson and Jennifer Filipowicz. Their feedback coaxed me to scale back details that would have confused readers.

My writers' critiquing group consists of smart and creative individuals who provided me with invaluable ideas. They are Linda Cassidy, Sharon Clare, Norma Meldrum and Carole-Ann Olsen, all gifted writers in different genres, from whom I learn so much.

A special word of gratitude must go to a brilliant psychotherapist, Dr. Beal, who helped me overcome childhood trauma and embark on a journey of positive change and recovery.

I would also like to thank Candace Havens' HelpMeEdit agency. The assigned editor helped shorten my first draft. Then, six years on, I was fortunate to find Beth Bruno, a caring and experienced professional who not only helped me further refine my manuscript but who also stayed in touch with useful information and advice.

Others that influenced me in some way in my worldview or writing were, in no particular order, Drs. Jennifer Levine, John Baird, Heather Jackson and J. Barbara Rose (my most memorable professors at the University of Toronto); Margaret Jackson; Greg Ioannou; Kathryn Wilms; Bernie Schilling, Anne-Marie O'Brien and Jill Perry. I am grateful, as well, for the kindness of extended family members.

Finally, my husband, David Tucker, who remains an invaluable source of support. As a media professor, he gave me new ideas for presenting my story and continued to encourage my writing, when I sometimes wanted to throw in the towel. His faith in me kept me going.

Proceeds from this book will be donated to charities.

For privacy concerns, I have changed most of the names, places and timelines that appear in this book. But behind Northingthorpe is a real town, and it is my wish that the true events described will offer hope and insight to others, knowing they are not alone.

Sheila Elsie Tucker

Start where you are. Use what you have. Do what you can.

—Arthur Ashe

For David

Preface

It's summer of 2010. I'm sitting cross-legged on a rug in my basement, pulling family memories out of a big cardboard box I'd kept closed for decades: a box full of Sixties memorabilia like the pendant with a small picture of The Beatles inside. There's a chain belt and a mod mini skirt my mother used to wear, as well as a psychedelic picture given to me as a kid.

Musty letters, old poems, tattered books, a half-finished piece of crotchet-work with the needle still pushed into it and a rickety pair of glasses—I can visualize Nana looking through them still. There's even a card signed in my childish hand to "Dear Mummy."

I'm holding a tiny handmade rag doll that Nana made for me, turning it over and over in my hands and now I raise it to my nose, hoping in vain to smell Nana's cologne. Instead, a slight whiff of mildew, stale stuffing and dust fill my nostrils. I close my eyes and imagine that I'm near her again. She was my rock during a very troubled time, at least for a while.

I begin reading several old letters from my mother to my grandparents, and from them to her, some sent shortly before I was born, in England, and others written while I was a child. They're a Pandora's Box of bittersweet memories that still clatter through my head quite often. I begin sobbing, unable to catch my breath. At this moment, I finally realize that I'll need help if I am ever to expel my demons once and for all.

A few days later, I get a referral to Dr. Beal, a psychologist near my home in Oakville, Canada, where I now live. I figure he is my last best hope to find peace. But I suppose I'm getting ahead of myself. If I am to make sense of any of this pain, I must start at the beginning.

1

It was very tempting. Just sneak away from this door. Forget the whole thing.

I looked longingly down the hall at the elevator. *Geez, am I really going to visit a shrink? Me? Now or never, kiddo.* I breathed in and turned the handle.

The receptionist finished her phone call and smiled at me. "Are you Mrs. Tucker? Love the gold sovereign." Cheerfully, she pointed to my ring. "Is that two heads on it?" She had a British accent similar to my own. I wondered what her story was. Like me, she had landed in Canada at some point and made it her home.

Feeling more comfortable, I moved my hand closer. "Can you make out who they are?"

"Is that Prince Charles and...oh."

"Yeah, and Lady Diana. These coins were a limited production to commemorate their engagement. Back in the days of innocence, eh? I wear it once in a while."

"Sheila? I'm Dr. Beal."

I swung around to face a tall man. Fair hair with a bit of grey. Blue eyes behind silver spectacles, a polite smile. I nodded mechanically, suddenly awkward, then shook his outstretched hand and followed him into his office. He gestured to four chairs in the corner opposite his own swivel-back.

"Sit wherever you like. So, how about you tell me why you're here, and then I'll give you the rundown on my credentials and experience. Let's see how I can help."

Oh boy, I thought. *What am I doing here...where the hell do I start? How do I start? At the beginning, I suppose.*

* * *

It was the late 1950s during a decade of post-war austerity, when my mother, Vivian, left school and began work. Jobs in her small, English seaside town were scarce, especially for young women from working class backgrounds with limited education. However, armed with an outgoing personality and good looks, she found a junior clerk position in Middlesbrough.

Vivian quickly found herself on the wrong side of her fellow workers: two frumpish, older secretaries. Perhaps they envied her girlish prettiness. Maybe they resented her exuberance. The two women made my mother's life miserable from day one. No matter how carefully she filed reports, she wasn't efficient enough; no matter how politely she answered the phone, she was never professional enough. Even a typo brought sarcasm raining down on her.

The secretaries watched Vivian like hawks. The moment she finished one chore they loaded her with more, like a farm donkey, before she could catch her breath, and they left her buried in work while they took long smoke breaks. In the summer she was left alone in the office while they enjoyed packed lunches in the park. Vivian worked harder and quicker, hoping they'd finally accept her, but nothing made any difference. They were the evil sisters to her Cinderella. Isolated and sad, she sat on a train, then bus, for an hour in the morning, worked in this environment all day, and then commuted home.

Mr. Dickson's attentions cheered her. When she brought the accountant his mail, he'd smile and compliment her, and before long he was chatting to her as a peer. Vivian felt flattered that such a mature, important man—Mr. Dickson being in his mid-thirties and in management—considered her worthy for conversation. She began daydreaming about him on the bus home and mentally replayed all his admiring glances and comments about her lovely blue eyes. To her, he became boyishly handsome. By the time they kissed, Vivian was already half in love. Soon he was "Spencer," at least when they were alone. The office became bearable whenever he was there, and she learned to switch off the bitchiness of the two secretaries.

I have no idea whether these women suspected the affair, but my mother always said they were cruel long before her entanglement with Spencer. I do believe their meanness contributed to the lonely girl falling eagerly into the welcoming arms of the boss. Likely, she mistook his attention for compassion, fell in love and allowed herself to be seduced.

I suspect Spencer wasn't being all that kind or concerned about the office bullying. Attracted to the new recruit in a time before workplace harassment policies, he simply homed in. His mutterings about a bad marriage allowed Vivian to imagine a shared future, and although she knew the affair was wrong, she convinced herself he'd leave his unhappy union.

It was when she told him of her pregnancy that he cooled off. He suggested she get the child adopted. Terrified, Vivian said she couldn't bring herself to tell her family—think of the stigma in rural England in the 1950s—and asked him to help her find an abortionist. To his credit, Spencer stressed the danger of back-alley abortions, and how girls often perished either during or shortly after these illegal operations, the victims of profiteers with wire coat hangers. In the end, he managed to talk her out of the idea, even though it would have made his life easier, for had she died his wife might never have eventually discovered his dalliance.

Soon after, seventeen-year-old Vivian read that drinking gin could sometimes induce a miscarriage. She confessed to me years later that she bought a bottle of alcohol and guzzled most of it. She remembered vomiting afterward and, needless to say, it didn't work. She tried another old wives' tale that claimed hot baths caused miscarriages. Night after night she steeped in near-scalding water but that didn't work either.

Had my mother been successful, my life would have begun and ended as an embryo, flushed away down a toilet. Perhaps I understood this instinctively, even as a little girl. For a long time I wished I hadn't been born, feeling I was simply a nuisance to everyone around me.

I was eight when I asked where I'd come from and Mum decided I was old enough to know the truth. "I was forced to tell my parents about the pregnancy," she told me. "But to my relief they stood by me. They truly loved all their children unconditionally."

I remember her stroking my hair as she recounted the next part of the story.

"Your grandad's brother, my uncle Bill, lived way up north with his wife Sheila. They opened their doors to me and I left town to wait for the birth." She smiled. "Sheila and Bill were childless and decided they'd adopt the baby. Everything seemed taken care of. I stayed three months, and my parents sent lots of letters, telling me how everyone missed me."

In one letter, Vivian's mother included the lyrics from a Rodgers and Hammerstein song and asked her daughter to read the words carefully. "Keep up hope, Viv," she wrote. "Everything will be alright—you are not alone, you have us."

Like my mum, I have since read those words many times and drawn hope from their simple message, which was to hold your head high when you're walking through a storm, even though your dreams are tossed in the wind. "Don't be afraid of the dark," the song said. It was called *You'll Never Walk Alone*.

"What I didn't anticipate was wanting to keep the baby. In hospital, miles away from home, I stared at you and knew I did not want my little girl adopted. I just couldn't be parted forever from you, She-she. I realized I needed to talk to my mum and dad, but not by writing letters. And with scarcely a penny to spare, my parents didn't own a telephone. They still don't." She sighed. "The nurses agreed to care for you whilst I took the train. I returned two days later to pack my things and head home with you."

Sheila and Bill were heartbroken for they had already planned the baby's bedroom and bought clothes for their soon-to-be-adopted child. Now, suddenly, they had to contend with the token gesture of being godparents. Vivian named me after her aunt and mother, so I became Sheila Elsie.

Vivian's relationship with her aunt and uncle remained strained ever afterwards. Sheila and Bill visited us in Northingthorpe twice a year from then on, but generally timed their trips for when my mother was not around. They took me for ice cream or to the park, and I recall many a time I'd glance up to catch Auntie Sheila gazing longingly at me. I never quite understood why until I learned this history at age eight, after which I always felt badly for them when they visited. I felt responsible for my godparents' wistfulness, and I was sure to always make a fuss of them and blow kisses when they left.

After my birth, my mother stayed with her family for over a year, but although family life was loving and supportive, she realized the need to move away from town gossip. Insecure, she married the first man who asked. Her family begged her not to, for they all disliked the whiny, egotistical good-for-nothing they felt Terry to be. A 20-year-old from Manchester, he was convalescing in our seaside town due to a bout of tuberculosis. The two headed to his home city to find work, intending to fetch me at a later date.

At age one I was left with my grandparents, uncles and aunt, and so I had almost no memories of my mother when she came for occasional visits.

I didn't lack attention with my teenaged uncles and aunt around: Bobby, Ed, Antony and Eleanor. I went to the park and the beach with Eleanor. Bobby and Ed bounced me on their knees and played their records, and I learned to talk by singing alongside them to the hits of the Everly Brothers and Elvis. By the time I was three they were taking me with them to the Go Kart track near the beach, where I sat between their knees on the roofless Lotus-style racecars. These were fast, noisy and exciting, and I hugged my uncles' legs as we zigzagged the track at high speed. I screamed but loved it even as they took sharp bends that almost had me airborne.

Nana was where I went for quieter times: cuddles and stories. Her voice was like a soft velvet cushion. Her hair was white silk. Other times I sat near Grandad, and he fed me runner beans he'd grown from seed. We lived in a rented century-old, large-roomed brick house with ivy growing up the side. Felicity Close was not only a cul-de-sac, it was also a narrow flagstone alley, lush with bushes, wildflowers, small trees, and the pretty gardens of the other five houses one passed before reaching ours. Vehicles were impossible; this was a pedestrian-only path. The peace and quiet was like something you would read in Wordsworth.

The one sound I do remember was from our nearby railway station, whose occasional steam trains tooted a warning before chugging off. Their horns had a distinct bellow, simultaneously high pitched and low. Occasionally my uncles walked me through our alley and along the adjoining road, at the end of which they perched me on a wooden fence bordering grassland of the railway property. Together we watched smoke in the near distance billowing from chimneys of these locomotives as coupling rods began to rise and fall in unison with the turning of giant wheels. I was fascinated by these side rods, which had a peculiar up-and-down movement, rather like the seesaw I sat on in the park, whilst at the same time they moved from side to side. As the rods began to move faster they were a blur of movement. At the same time, the wheel spokes, moving clockwise, appeared to change direction and spin anti-clockwise, a phenomenon explained to me by my uncles as an optical illusion. At three, I wasn't sure what "optical illusion" meant, but I understood it to mean "magic."

Indeed there was something magical about steam trains and even the diesels that were more common in my day: the smell of burning coal similar to fireplaces in our house; the occasional shriek of a moving metal bit demanding a drink of oil; the scream of the station master's whistle encouraging commuters to hurry; bogie-carts piled with mysterious freight, and carriage windows filled with friendly passengers who responded in kind to the enthusiastic little girl who blew kisses from the fence.

There was more magic in Grandad's garden, a mosaic of sparkling color. Sometimes I stood in the middle of his little winding path to gaze rapturously at his flowers, mostly taller than I. Grandad, lean and bronzed, spent a lot of time tending his beloved plants, aided by his eager little apprentice. My job was to guard a growing collection of accidentally dug-up earthworms until he was ready to return them to the soil. This employment usually consisted of my gently playing with them.

Nana, now unable to walk very much, always sat in the same place: a comfy chair with threadbare arms in the corner of the living room at the side of the fireplace. From here, draped in a paisley pinafore and with handmade slippers warming her swollen feet, she could enjoy the warmth of the fire on cold days. She could also turn and peek through the window at the abundant garden. She enjoyed sitting here with balls of colored wool at her side, her crochet needle at the ready, making shawls or cardigans. At the end of each day, I climbed onto her lap and fell asleep while she sang. I learned the words and we sang along at about the ages of three and fifty-three, in unison: "Golden slumbers kiss your eyes, Smiles await you when you rise."

My days consisted of such essential rituals as waving to Grandad as he cycled off to work and helping Nana roll pastry. As well, I had fun with a little girl who lived in the big house on the other side of the cul-de-sac. The Williamsons' property ran the full length from Sycamore Road, where Felicity Close began, up to our house, so it was six house-lengths long and surrounded by a tall wooden fence. I could peer through gaps in the wood and was tantalized by an out-of-reach swing, a red pedal-car and other exotic toys. My childish nosiness was how I met Sarah.

One day, peeking longingly at that swing through a crack, a small face crowded my vision, and a hazel-brown eye peeped back at me. Sarah giggled and poked her finger through a hole. I tickled her fingertip and we both laughed. Soon I received invitations to play with her, and at last got a ride on the swing. Sarah was almost two and I was nearly three when we met, and for more than a year we danced, chuckled, rolled over each other and shared toys. I didn't have many to share, but it didn't matter. We threw balls, dug in her sandbox and took dolls for walks. We kissed each other's cheeks, sang nursery rhymes and hugged. This was as close as I ever came to having a sister in childhood, and I had her for a whole year.

My uncle Bobby had a newspaper boy's bike, the kind with a square metal frame built into the front of the handlebars, into which a tray of newspapers was placed. I was just the right size to sit in the tray, and Bobby, tall and strong, with red hair and a Roman nose like Grandad's, would tuck me in front and pedal along on errands. I'd wave to folks and ask Bobby to pedal faster.

Other times I sat on Eleanor's knee to play with her necklace. She was tall, just like Bobby, Ed, Antony and Grandad. Only Nana and Mummy were shorter. Everyone's eyes were blue, but Nana's and Mummy's were the bluest.

My toy box upstairs was an ottoman with a brocaded lid. I pulled out balls or my rag dolls and took them downstairs to play at Nana's feet. At the end of the day, I went to sleep on my cot in Eleanor's room. Ed and Antony slept next door. Both bedrooms were huge. Bobby had small-but-private quarters along the corridor past the bathroom. The landing over the stairs had a spare bed and my mother slept here when she came to visit, although I have no vivid memories about her from this period.

My uncles' record player was kept in the hall, and I sang along with the recordings to words I loved but didn't quite understand. Thus, "Hey, bird dog, you're on the wrong trail," became a part of my vernacular, as did other aspects of contemporary teenage life, such as "winkle pickers," which I thought meant shoes in general (Nana, dear, shall I tuck your winkle pickers under the bed?), and "Bobbysocks" were, I thought, my darling Bobby's laundered socks. Beehives were not, in those days, something fuzzy insects lived in; they were, in my mind, only the big hairstyles favored by Eleanor.

*   *   *

"There is a reason I'm describing all this," I told Dr. Beal during that first visit.

I'd arrived reluctantly, skeptically, at his office and wasn't yet sure whether I even liked him. Wasn't he one of those privileged, well-educated guys with an easy life? How would he possibly get it? A life like mine? How could he extricate the shrapnel embedded in my head and my heart?

"You probably wonder why I'm here. You'll find out. But I need you to know how it started...how happy I once was."

My mother and me

2

Many days the house was empty except for Nana and me.

My uncles and aunt went to work or class. Grandad was a janitor at the junior school and supplemented his income by gardening. He was tall and very slim, possibly due to all the physical labour he put in, and Nana was short and plump. I regarded them both as cuddly.

I followed Nana around each morning, except when *Watch With Mother* was on television. Then I sat rapturously watching Andy Pandy, Teddy and Looby Loo jump out of the ottoman at the end of their owner's bed. They were toys that came to life when no one was around. I followed their adventures, then the show always ended with them back in their box, slowly ducking out of view as the lid closed. They waved goodbye. I waved back, secure in the knowledge I'd see them again soon.

After our daily dose of "Watch With Nana," as I called it, we headed to the kitchen to make soup for my uncles and Grandad, who popped home for lunch. This, like everything, was a laborious affair for my grandmother, who could only shuffle around by pushing a wooden chair in front of her for support due to her weak legs.

"Come on, She-she." Nana slowly hoisted herself from her armchair. "Want to help me make lunch for Grandad? He'd be so happy. You're very good at buttering bread, you know."

Leaning heavily on the chair-back while pushing it ahead, she stepped forward with one leg, then dragged the other, hands gripping tightly. Step, drag, step, drag.

"I'm coming." I sometimes grabbed another chair and followed, pushing it as best I could even though it was too big for me. We moved across the long living room in this fashion, with me stepping and dragging and swaying as I trailed her.

One day Eleanor was home. "Sheila, stop, it's not nice."

Nan turned her head. "What's the matter?"

"She's mimicking you, Mum," Eleanor told her.

Nan shrugged with the experience of a woman who has brought up several children.

"She's only a child, Eleanor dear. Children learn by copying. She doesn't mean anything by it." And she continued on her way.

"Nana," I said. "Can I keep on?"

"Of course, darling. Come on, we'll race."

After that, I often grabbed a chair when she did, and we'd cross the floor side-by-side and shuffle into the kitchen. Now and then we'd race. I sometimes beat her to the kitchen, but more often I pretended to tire out so she could win. Then she'd be delighted and say, "Hooray, I won this time."

Nana and Grandad slept in a large bed downstairs because of her disability and, in fact, the move to Felicity Close had helped prolong her independence thanks to there being a powder room on the ground floor: rare in most English houses in those days. Nana was getting older, and the polio that almost carried her away as a small child had destroyed her left leg, which now hung almost uselessly.

When Eleanor was home, she often took me down a couple of streets to the beach and one time bought me a tinsel windmill…a pinwheel, some call it nowadays. I can still see my aunt in my mind's eye, her flaxen hair blowing, toes in the sand as she carried her sandals.

"Hold up your windmill and see what happens."

"Look, Eleanor!" I gripped the skinny stick tightly as the bracing North Sea wind grabbed my new toy, the red and blue blades whipping around, blurring into purple. "Listen too. It hums."

"You can show it to Nana. Time to go home, She-she."

"Come back tomorrow?"

"Yep."

Eleanor took my hand and we strolled over the beach road and around the corner. I stopped to yank dandelions poking from a crack and we continued along the narrow path. I picked a buttercup from near the fence.

"Hello, darling," said Nana. "What lovely flowers. And what's this?"

"Eleanor bought it for me. It goes round and round. But in here it doesn't move."

"Yes, it does," said Eleanor. "Blow on it hard."

I gathered all my breath and blew at the windmill. Sure enough, it rotated.

"It's magic. Look, Nana, I can do magic."

I held my windmill high and ran fast through the house. This did the same trick. Around it went.

"Hello, Bobby. Are you finished at work? See this windmill and watch it spin."

"Wow, aren't you clever. You're a magical fairy." Bobby smiled.

"Dinnertime, Grandad? I only want chicken. Okay, carrots please. Bobby, help me make a face again...yes, mash can be the hair. Peas for the eyes...ha ha, carrot nose! A mouth? Oh yes, peas again, make a smile. That's you, Bobby, it's just like you."

Later, I sat on Nana's lap, facing over her shoulder, being rocked by her. I stroked the wallpaper pattern as she sang to me.

My nana is the best in the world. And Grandad is nice too, and Eleanor and Bobby and Ed and...I'm very tired. But I don't want to sleep. I want to stay here. Nana is like a comfy pillow. Tomorrow I'll help Grandad again. I'll pick weeds and dig soil. Maybe I'll make a soil castle, like I make sandcastles at the beach.

Darling Nana. Let me sing with you. Golden slumbers kiss your eyes...Nana, your cheek is wet.

I was nearly four when my grandparents told me Mummy was again coming to visit.

I was always glad to see her, although sometimes I was also glad when she left. Sometimes she could shout in a scary way. She arrived looking lovely as always in a bright yellow and grey dress.

Her rose-pink lipstick, her white teeth, her blue eyes and long lashes reminded me of one of my pretty dolls.

"My lovely girl," she said in her good-mood voice, beaming with happiness. She picked me up.

"Twirl me?" I asked. She grabbed my hands and swung me around, then stopped and I tried to stand, swaying dizzily, chuckling at how the room seemed to be moving.

Mummy and Nana and I had tea, and together began dinner preparations. Nana let me butter the bread. I hoped Mummy would stay a long time for this visit. Later, she read me to sleep and woke me early the next morning.

"La la la. Te dee dum dum. Guess what, She-she, we're going on a ride."

"Is Nana coming?"

"Yes, Nana's coming."

"Okay, but I want to take Rosebud."

Rosebud was a pretty plastic doll Nana had given me a few days before. She had pale curly hair and eyes that closed when I laid her down.

"Yes, you can take Rosebud. We'll be taking your clothes and your other toys too."

"Why?"

"Oh…in case you happen to want them."

"No, I only want Rosebud. I'll see my other toys when I come back this afternoon."

But Mummy still had a lot of bags.

*   *   *

It's the Swinging Sixties in England. My uncles Bobby, Ed and Antony, all teenagers, are listening to Top Ten songs on the radio. The Shirelles' *Will You Love Me Tomorrow* comes on and Ed dances with me, his large, grown-up hands holding my tiny ones, waltzing me around the living room as I wait to go on that ride with my grandparents and mother.

"Come on," Mummy calls from the hallway. "Let's put your shoes on."

I stop dancing and run to her. It's thrilling to be going to the train station. We leave the house after rushed goodbyes with my uncles. The porters help Nana onto the train, along with her fold-up wheelchair. Grandad climbs in and pulls me up. Mummy hands him the luggage and we all sit on two long seats facing each other. The carriage stinks of nicotine and Grandad opens the window to let air in. I smell the sea even though we can't quite see our town's beach from the station. A whistle blows. The train comes to life.

"Hooray!" I jump up and down, excited to be onboard. Soon we arrive at a massive station—much bigger than our little one in Northingthorpe—and wait on another platform. A different train pulls in and Mummy tells me to say goodbye to Nana and Grandad.

"Why?" I ask.

"Darling, I have to go home and cook," Nana tells me. "Don't worry, you'll be back soon. Go with Mummy."

I grab Nana's hand. "You're coming too," I say. "We're all going, aren't we?"

"She-she," Mummy says, crouching in front of me. "We'll come back later. Come on, come with me."

I've never been anywhere without Nana. I cling to her hand. "I thought we were all going out for the day."

"We're just coming this far," Grandad says. "Let me help you get on the train. Wave to us from there." He holds me for a last hug with Nana before lifting me up the steps of the train. "Mummy will take you somewhere nice. We'll see you soon."

I put my thumb in my mouth and let Mummy carry me through the looming door.

"Bye then, Nana. Bye, Grandad."

Mummy holds me steady at the carriage window, and I hear a guard's whistle. I blow kisses in between sucking my thumb, and Nana, down on the platform, waves from her wheelchair and smiles.

Grandad is not in my mind's-eye picture at this point. It is Nana I remember: my rock, my dearest, my loving Nana, who cuddles me so well and who reads me to sleep each night. I'm sad she's not coming on the day out, for I'm used to her always being nearby.

"See you soon."

She keeps looking at me, and waves again. Then the train begins to move.

That whole day is seared into my mind: listening to the music, dancing with my uncles, and Nana getting smaller as the train carries me away. And all these years later, I know and remember this as the day everything changed.

Aged 3

3

"I don't recall much about the trip, Dr. Beal. I'm not sure I'd ever been on a train before, except to be brought to Northingthorpe as a newborn. It felt strange to be onboard, even though I'd watched trains go by so often."

It was the second visit of my venture into counseling. With the aura of a kindly schoolteacher, my psychologist sat in a swivel chair with his back to a desk pressed against the far wall. He had recapped my story from the week before and asked me to continue.

"I think I know where we're going with this, but I still need to hear it from you, as much as you feel is relevant," he said.

"Oh, you'll hear a lot." I sighed as I folded my arms. "There's so much I haven't forgotten, although I wish I could." I watched him turn a page in his notebook. Then he reached to pull down a blind as the sun began to shine in.

"Nana told me years later that she and Grandad insisted on coming with us on the local train to Middlesbrough station, where the other train was to take my mother and me across the country. Everyone agreed it was best to let me think I was on a day's outing or else I'd have struggled all the way, so when I asked Nana why she wasn't coming on the larger train with Mummy and me, she said she couldn't but that she'd see me later. The train pulled out and I waved one last time. That was the point Nana broke down and cried, she told me years later. On the return trip to Northingthorpe, a woman sat opposite with a little girl about my age, and Nana sobbed all the way home while Grandad, stoic as always, tried to comfort her."

"Sheila, what about you? Let's leave your grandparents for now and get back to what was happening with you."

"What I recall about my own trip is it took a long, long time. I fell asleep, and when I awoke I wondered where my cot was. I must have been making a noise, because my mother sternly told me to be quiet. I sat thinking how glad I'd be when we arrived home again.

"The journey came to an end, and she carried our things. We walked along a strange, foggy street. I felt alarmed because every single house was identical and there were no big trees at all. I didn't like this place. All the houses in Northingthorpe were different in some way, even the row houses. Nana and Grandad's was ivy-covered and had a green wooden porch. The Williamsons' home was stately and grand, made of cream brick. Sycamore Road and Felicity Close were full of unique houses. There were large porches or no porches, tall chimneys, small, fat chimneys, leaded windows or plain glass, lace curtains or velvet drapes. Door knockers ranged from a wrought iron lion's head to a brass Scottish thistle. Some houses were red brick, some yellow, others were stone or stucco."

I stopped a moment to recall my old neighbourhood. Then I sighed and continued.

"But here on the street I was now walking along with my mother, every house looked exactly the same. Red brick with small square windows and identical doors. Even the gardens were the same—treeless, sparse little lawns with weeds. No flowers anywhere. The sidewalk and road were similar shades of grey concrete."

Dr. Beal glanced up from his notes, astonished. "Quite the memory for a four year old. Are you certain you noticed all that? Just from walking along a street?"

"Oh, you'd be surprised at what I remember. I've always been good at recalling trivia, Lord knows why. And don't forget, I was in an unfamiliar place for the first time in my life so I was looking around as we walked."

* * *

I was stuck in a bad dream, alarmed at the sight of this sterile street, even more so when my mother opened one of the identical gates and led me into the stale-smelling entrance of one of the houses.

A television blared and a pale man with black hair and thick glasses sat in a patterned armchair. He stood up when we walked in, and Mummy told me this was Terry. He was going to be my daddy.

At age four, my concept of "dad" was that my uncles and aunt called Grandad "dad." Although I called him Grandad, I viewed him as my dad too. I may have said as much in my own childish way, because my mother and this man were very firm in that Terry was my dad. In the days to come I tried to remember this, but to his ire I mostly called him Terry, the same as my mother did. But that first evening, after being on an interminable journey for longer than I'd ever known possible, I wasn't in the mood for any more games. It was getting dark and I wanted to go home to bed. Mummy said, "You *are* home." I said I was not; this was not Nana and Grandad's house. Terry insisted I was to forget that house; this was my new home.

I felt my chest tighten. "But you said we were just out for the day. Let me go now. Nana will worry."

"Quit crying," the man shouted. "This is your house now. Get used to it!"

My mother took me into the kitchen, but I couldn't eat. She finally put me to bed in a strange room where a baby was sleeping on a cot.

The following morning I rose early and wandered into the hall. No one was in sight, and I pushed open a door only to find the same man I'd encountered the evening before lying on top of Mummy and hitting her with his body.

"Stop hurting my Mummy," I screamed and dashed over to push him off.

He grabbed me by the neck and shoved me. I fell choking onto the floor, but was up in an instant to save my mother from him. He continued to pound her with his torso.

"Stop it, Terry," my mother said. "I need to get up and deal with

with her."

By now I was back on the bed, pulling his arm. "Get off," I shouted.

"I ain't quitting till I've finished," Terry yelled at my mother, then he punched me in the stomach, making me roll away, gasping for breath. In pain, I backed into a corner of the room.

"Don't kill my Mummy," I screamed.

I sank to the floor, sobbing, while she continued to order him to stop. Eventually she was able to get out of bed. She crouched and stroked my hair. I hugged her for dear life, and she carried me out of the room while Terry hollered about what a horrid troublemaker I was.

A bit later he barged into my room, where my mother was helping me dress. "Don't you ever fucking enter our bedroom again, d'you hear?" He pointed at me and bared his teeth. "If you do, you'll be bloody sorry!"

"Terry, it's her first day here," my mother said. "Be easy on her. I'll give her some house rules." She looked at me. "He's right. We need privacy, and you mustn't come into our room."

"But he might hit you again," I said. "I don't want you to go into there again either."

"You're too young to understand," she replied. "I'm fine—he wasn't hurting me. Everything's okay, so come on. Jeanette's awake now and we'll all go downstairs."

I sat on a dining room chair stock-still, trying to be invisible while Terry fed the baby and glowered at me. Mummy washed the dishes and seemed happy enough, so I had to believe her. She wasn't injured, and I never entered their room again.

*   *   *

"Do you see now, Dr. Beal? Where I'm going with this?" I took off my glasses and polished them.

"I'm beginning to." He shifted in his seat. Middle-aged like me, he exuded aged wisdom cloaked by humility into the eight feet between us. "You were taken away from everything familiar, to live with a mother you scarcely knew and her husband, an unpleasant individual you'd never met."

"Everyone lied to me. They said I was on a day out. I couldn't understand why Nana let this happen. If this was all, it would be bad enough, but what happened next...damn, we're out of time and I'm sure you have another patient waiting. I'll tell you next week if that's okay? It's rather detailed."

As I arrived home I heard the church bell in the distance. Clang, clang, bong. Three o'clock. I opened a bottle of wine and drank half of it. *Sod it*, I thought. *Sod it all!*

The next day I cancelled the following week's appointment and decided to stop going.

My mind was a mess. Tears streamed endlessly from my eyes, fury burned in my veins and I stared at walls a lot. I found it difficult at work to behave as though nothing was wrong and at home I watched TV only to find I hadn't taken anything in.

After three weeks I was back in the chair in Dr. Beal's office. "Continue where you left off last time," he said.

* * *

I don't recall much about the first week following my arrival in the house in Manchester or how I settled in—if "settle" is the right word. Truth be told, I never, ever, settled in. I was simply forced to live there.

I think even if my mother had been a gentler, more patient person, even if Terry had been a regular, nice kind of guy, I'd still have yearned for the house in Northingthorpe, for Nana sitting in her corner and Grandad puttering in the garden. As it was, I lived in fear the whole time.

The one way I can use the word "settled" is that we settled into a routine. We got up in the morning, my mother dashed around to get dressed and head out to her office job five days a week, while Terry, unemployed, stayed home with me and the child they'd had together,

Jeanette. My mother's wages supplemented their welfare money, but failed to give her any independence. She had no education beyond age fifteen, the normal age for working class children to leave school, and wages paid to women were low.

During the week, I hardly saw my mother except at breakfast. On weekends she was busy with household chores. Terry wasn't home as much on weekends; perhaps he watched soccer or visited his sisters.

A childproof gate appeared, and on rainy weekends Jeanette and I were trapped in the living room while my mother did housework. I hated being stuck in there. It was often for hours. I didn't play with Jeanette; I either watched television or amused myself at the opposite end of the room.

One day I needed the bathroom and called for my mother to open the gate.

"Can't you see I'm busy doing laundry?"

In those days, this was a slow process involving a cumbersome machine.

"But I really need to go now, Mummy."

"You'll have to wait, I'm tied up."

I sat on the floor in front of the television. I finally wet myself and the linoleum I was sitting on, took off my soaking pants and began to flip pages of a picture book. I was quite absorbed in the pictures when my mother grabbed me and hit me hard.

"Look what you've done. Peed on the floor, you bad girl."

"No, no, that is not fair, Mummy." I stamped my feet in rage. "I told you I needed to go. You wouldn't let me out."

"Just shut up. You're a damn nuisance."

I learned how to climb over the kiddie-gate, but the day I did I was threatened so severely that I just stayed in the living room sucking my thumb. Often I didn't play at all. I dreamed of being rocked on Nana's knee or of being taken to the beach by Eleanor. There was no beach here. Beyond this street were more streets, all identical to this one.

On sunny days I was allowed in the garden and eventually to

play at some kids' home around the corner, but I missed Sarah and wished I could sit on her swing.

The first time I walked back home by myself after playing with these kids, I couldn't figure out which was our house because of the hideous sameness of them all. Lost, I finally went to the wrong door and started crying. The woman who lived there seemed to know who I was and led me to the right gate.

I asked for Nana a lot, but Mummy always got angry, and Terry forced me to say "This Is My Home, This Is My Home." I'd say it, scared of what would happen if I didn't, but shortly after, I would be back to saying, "Where is Nana? Let me see her."

There was no phone and my grandparents didn't have one either. Not that speaking to Nana by phone would have done much good. I wanted to be back in Northingthorpe with her.

Finally, Terry yelled, "Your nana doesn't want you, because you're a horrid little brat. She hates you. So shut the fuck up."

Shaken, I went upstairs. Sitting alone, I wondered: *Why does Nana hate me? Why doesn't she want me anymore? Is it because I lost one of her crochet hooks?*

I closed my eyes tight, trying to send my thoughts to Nana, wherever she was.

Please don't hate me, Nana. I'll be good. I'll do whatever you say. I love you, Nana. Please don't hate me.

Nana didn't hear me, or if she did, she didn't come for me. I didn't want Mum to hate me either, so I tried to be good, but everything was new and confusing, such as the time Terry brought a new box of cereal to the table. My mother fed Jeanette in the high chair, and when I looked at my dish, a ball of string was sitting in it. I didn't have any idea how it had got there, and I sat staring at it in amazement. Terry poured milk on this string and told me to eat. I knew I couldn't. I'd choke. It would be like eating one of Nana's balls of wool.

I said, "No thank you, I'm not hungry."

"You're not wasting it, get it eaten," said Mummy.

I stared at her, then back at the bowl. "I can't eat that."

"You can and you will," said Terry. "No nonsense from you. Eat it."

"No, thank you."

"Come on, She-she, eat." Mummy was in a good mood and tried to be nice.

However, I couldn't bring myself to eat string. It would taste awful and stick in my throat. Silently, I shook my head. Terry slammed down his cup, grabbed a spoon with one hand and my hair with the other. He tried to force the spoon into my mouth, but I kept my teeth clenched, until he dug harder, cutting my lip. I opened my mouth to scream, and he shoved the string into my mouth. I immediately spat it out and became hysterical, screaming and crying. Mummy came over and pushed him away.

"Not so hard," she said.

"Fucking hell." Terry stomped away.

When I finally calmed down, Mummy asked why I wouldn't at least try it.

"I can't eat a ball of string," I sobbed. "I'll choke."

She closed her eyes. "Christ, she thinks we're feeding her string. Dear, it's not string. It's called shredded wheat. It's nice. Go ahead and try some."

But it was too late. I couldn't eat a thing and began to hate sitting with them at breakfast. I preferred to be on my own, because Mummy paid more attention to Jeanette, and Terry always spoke kindly to Jeanette. They eventually gave up trying to make me eat breakfast.

I learned what to expect each morning: everyone washing and dressing, Jeanette and me left playing—well, she'd be playing; I sat on the couch, dreading the day. Mum dashed off to work. Terry watched television for a while then took Jeanette upstairs for her nap. When he came down, he'd have a look in his eyes I came to recognize—glassy, an unmistakable leer behind the black-framed glasses. Although I didn't know the word "leer" then, I knew that expression meant he was going to get me.

Every day he eyed me like that, sitting in his patterned chair, beckoning me over. I knew I had to obey; it would be worse for me if I didn't. I'd stand in front of him. He'd take a slipper off his foot, pull down my knickers, lift my dress and bend me over his knee. He spanked me with that slipper until his arm was tired with the exertion, pounding, repeating slap after slap on my buttocks until I was screaming, until I simply couldn't scream any more, until I was choking in my cries. Then he would fling me like a limp doll onto the floor, smirking.

"That's for being a bad girl. Nasty little fucker."

*   *   *

"This is the beginning of the abuse you mentioned in our first meeting."

Dr. Beal looked at me seriously. I was sure my bitterness was palpable whilst recounting these events and that he could see it.

"You've said you feel angry about many things. I could arrange to have you see one of my colleagues instead, a woman."

"Why?" I glared at him. "Don't you want to be bothered with me? Am I too horrible for you?"

"Not at all. But how do you feel about men today? In general, I mean. Some women prefer to discuss these things with another woman."

"Oh. There are good and bad in both sexes. I have no problem with men."

"You're comfortable talking to me, then?"

"About as comfortable as I would be with anyone. Yes."

"Okay. But Sheila, I want to delve more into what just happened. You asked if I don't want to be bothered with you and whether you are too awful for me. Why?"

I shrugged, but he continued to press me.

"Think about it. Why did you presume that?"

"Dunno...perhaps because as soon as I begin talking about the dirty stuff, you suddenly want to shunt me off to someone else."

"Why was that your first thought, and not that I wondered if you may be more at ease with a woman, or some other possibility?"

He waited calmly while I thought about it, so I tried prying into my reactions.

"Look, for most of my life, people have had no patience with me. I was just a nuisance. I guess deep down I still believe everyone sees me as a nasty little fucker. Why would you be any different?"

"But..."

"I know I was angry when I was telling you all this. Suddenly you're seeing under the surface, the real me, and you don't like what you find. So you want to stop seeing me."

"Here's the thing, Sheila. I'm a professional. I've seen and heard a lot in my career. Nothing you told me gives me any negative opinions about you. Oh, and you're paying me, for goodness sake." He laughed and then nodded reassuringly. "I'd want to keep my clients, wouldn't I?"

"I'm sure you can pick and choose your clients."

"Is it possible you jumped to conclusions because of a lifelong habit of blaming yourself?"

I sighed. "I guess I'm just used to people not liking me. Thinking I'm an idiot or worse."

"We'll have to work on these thought patterns of yours." He nodded. "All in good time."

I relaxed as I realized I liked this guy. He was patient. He was polite. I proffered a smile.

Dr. Beal smiled back. "Unfortunately, our hour's up. Shall I see you next week, Sheila?"

"Sure."

I picked up my bag and waved goodbye.

4

I can't remember how long it was before Terry's fetish evolved into perversion, but one morning after the daily beating, he kneeled in front of me and unzipped his pants.

From then on every day he'd grab my little hand and wrap it around his organ, forcing me to rub hard. I had no idea what this thing was. I only knew it looked like a pork sausage. I didn't understand why he kept it stuffed into his trousers, or why I was meant to stroke it. It also felt strange to me that Terry was transformed at these times from an angry man who beat me into a trembling, gentle man talking sweetly, telling me what a good girl I was. These changes in him scared me. He seemed out of breath as if running too fast, and suddenly liked me, when just a short time before he had hated me, slippered me, screamed at me.

Although I was only four, I intuitively knew what I was doing was very wrong.

Terry obviously approved of my caressing his sausage, but there was something sick about his manner at these times, and I felt there was something about the thing in his pants that was dangerous, dirty and evil. But I stood still as a statue and passively allowed his hand to guide mine, firmer, faster. I was too afraid of more punishment if I resisted. And I gradually learned that if I reached out voluntarily at these times, he was even more pleased, and so I pretended to smile, and he grinned back and stroked my cheek—showing the gentleness I craved instead of violence—and I rubbed hard and acted as if I was happy, all the while numb and sick.

Often he left me alone after this morning ritual, and I don't much recall what the rest of my day consisted of. I suppose I ate lunch and dinner, or I would have starved to death. I do know that when Jeanette was up and about, I had to give way to her on everything. If she wanted my doll, I had to let her have it. If she knocked over my brick building, I was not to make a fuss. I was never to bother her. I learned to play apart from her as much as possible, and especially to keep my doll hidden from her sight. I couldn't bear seeing her take Rosebud, my only link to Nana, and I still thought of Northingthorpe all the time. I just wished I knew how to find my way back there.

I cried sometimes and asked to go home. This angered Terry, who often shut me in the bedroom, where I panicked like a sparrow trapped in an attic. Terry and his daughter were downstairs and I was alone, staring out of the window at the houses across the street. One day it occurred to me that if I shouted loudly enough, Nana might hear me and come. The window was open for air, so I leaned out and shouted as hard as I could, "Naannnaaaaaa!"

I hoped my voice would carry to wherever she was. Or maybe Eleanor would hear me from the shops, or Grandad, gardening, might say, "Ah, there's our She-she calling," and come running. I gazed from the bedroom window, craning my neck to see along the street. "Naannnaaaa." I wanted so much to see Bobby riding up to put me in his bike box and carry me off. "Naannnaaaaaaa."

I was yanked in by Terry, who closed the window and hit me hard. "She can't hear you. You're wasting your time, stupid. Don't do that again."

I thought sooner or later she would hear me and waited for a day Terry, Jeanette and I were in the back garden. I went in and straight to my bedroom window at the other side of the house and began calling. Terry caught me again and this time threw me over to my bed, where I hit the wall before bouncing down. My shoulder throbbed. I never used that window for calling Nana again. I did, however, come up with a new idea.

I decided to jump out of the window and run away to find Northingthorpe, thinking that because I was shut in the bedroom for such long stretches, Terry wouldn't realize I was gone until I was already safely back at Felicity Close. I clambered onto the windowsill and looked down. It seemed a long drop to the garden below. I shuddered and backed away, but I then stared at the houses across the road and focused my gaze beyond their roofs. Somewhere over there was Nana and Grandad's house. Somewhere out there. I jumped.

The hard, dry earth pounded my legs, but I managed to get up and limp to the gate, eager to search for Nana's house.

To my horror I saw a man running toward me. A woman with shopping bags came at me from the opposite direction. Both reached me at the same time. "Are you okay? Are you hurt?" I shook my head and made to walk off, but the woman restrained me, the man knocked on the door, and the next thing I knew Terry was bending over me, talking tenderly in the way he always did when others were present. The woman explained how she saw me fall from an upstairs window and offered to find a doctor, but Terry refused. "It's okay, I'll take over from here." He carried me inside.

Later, I thought about my escape attempt and realized I needed to ensure nobody was watching. I didn't jump again for a while, because my legs were sore, but finally, after a particularly bad morning with Terry, I found myself again sitting on the windowsill.

I waited until no one was walking by. Still, I was very afraid. I knew it was a long way down and remembered the pain in my legs. I sat, willing myself to jump to freedom, but hesitating. The image of Nana came into my mind. There she was, holding her arms out to me. I looked at the ground again, and thought, if I just sit here, I won't hurt my legs. Suddenly I found myself thinking of Terry's slipper and Terry's sausage. I jumped.

This time it was worse. I landed awkwardly and my head hit an old brick. Terry came out and tried to stand me on my feet, but I was incapable of standing. He carried me into the house, and I remember nothing else about that day. Perhaps I passed out. But I was never able to open that window again. From then on, it was fastened shut.

A few weeks after my last escape attempt, I was enrolled in a school full of what seemed like noisy young ruffians. Terry walked me over and picked me up until I learned my way. There were short cuts: passages between the rows of houses, then a walk across a wasteland of tall weeds.

I once asked the teacher how I could get home, meaning Nana and Grandad's, but she thought I meant where I was now living and asked a neighbouring boy to take me home after school. He was surprised and led me to my gate, asking how come I didn't know where my house was. He'd seen me walk to and from school. I tried to explain that I wanted my other house, but he looked blankly at me and left.

Another time, after the school day was done, I just couldn't bear the thought of going back to Terry—by now, he had switched his ritual with me to the afternoons. I never saw my mother after school, only him, and he always put me to bed before she returned from work, so this day I crouched to hide in the middle of the weedy wasteland. Other kids passed on the gravel trail on their way home, but I knew Terry would never find me. I sat there a long time, much preferring my solitude in an unkempt field to being with him. After a while, a boy from my street approached.

"Your dad wants you home right now."

"I don't want to go," I said. "He won't find me. I can sleep here."

"He asked if I'd seen you," said the boy. "I told him you were here."

"I'm not going!" I curled up on the dry grass.

The boy left but returned after a few minutes. "Your dad says you're to get home right now. If he has to walk over here, you're in big trouble. You'd better come."

I realized he was right—if Terry knew I was here, there was no point in staying. I walked alongside the boy.

"Why did you tell him where I was?"

"I didn't know you were hiding," he said. "It's a silly game, anyway."

It dawned on me that the boy just didn't get it, and I figured he'd never needed to hide from his family. I wondered why other kids seemed so content to walk into their homes. Didn't they dread the pain and horror? Was it only me at the receiving end of such treatment?

One time at school, knowing Mummy was home sick, I snuck out in between classes to be with her. When I opened the door, she and Terry were sitting at the dining table. He immediately screamed that I should be at school, but I looked only at Mummy. She came over, concerned, and knelt in front of me.

"Why did you leave?" she asked.

"I miss you."

She looked so sad at that moment, so very sad. She wrapped her arms around me.

"She mustn't do this, Viv. Get her back there right now. Don't encourage her!"

"Mummy, I knew you were home. I don't see you much...I only want to be with you awhile..."

"...it's just like I told you, Viv, she's always doing stuff like this...badly behaved little git...damn well knows she should be at school..."

"Okay, I'll walk her over." My mother led me out.

As we walked hand in hand over the weedy field, I suggested she and I run away to Northingthorpe. She shook her head quietly. I could tell she was miserable. I begged her; we would be happy at Nana's, I explained.

When we arrived at the school, she knelt in front of me. "She-she, I have a job and a baby. I can't just leave."

I sucked my thumb. "Can I stay off school just for today? Me and you could take a walk, Mummy. We could find a park with swings, maybe a beach and build sandcastles."

"No. You're to go back to class and not do this again. It's not allowed. Go!" She gave me a gentle shove.

I pushed one foot in front of the other, head lowered, as I walked to the school door. When I looked back, my mother waved, then walked away.

* * *

"So, you see, Dr. Beal, I was at his mercy all day, every week." I was incapable of describing Terry's practices in detail. I had told Dr. Beal only briefly that I was sexually abused; I simply couldn't put any of it into words. "I hardly saw my mother. I don't know why she bothered to drag me to Manchester at all. But I don't get why this is all bubbling up in me. Why now, after all these years?"

I stared out the office window, my fingers tapping the arm of the chair. This was my fourth session and I had been bouncing off the walls for the first three, alternately tearful, aggressive and defensive. It had taken until now for Dr. Beal to burrow through my force field, earn some of my trust and help me calm down.

"You experienced early childhood trauma, Sheila. You're not alone. An example would be the victims of residential schools here in Canada. Native children separated from family way back and forced to live under hostile conditions. Did you see the TV discussion on that a few weeks ago? Yes? Did you notice some of those people in tears as they spoke of what they went through decades before? It doesn't go away. You mentioned in our last session your sense of dissociation toward humanity in general. You don't need to feel guilty or puzzled; your reactions are quite common."

"I guess." I shifted my position and folded my arms. "By age seventeen I couldn't remain anywhere for more than a few months. I became a drifter, not just in England but far away, the more exotic the better. By my teens, I was averse to any long-term commitment. And I think my rootless, backpacking years originate from two events in particular. First, from being taken from my grandparents at age four. And second, the day I played truant to see my mother, the day I desperately wanted to spend time with her, quality time: an outing where we could laugh and play and forget our problems. Just have some fun. The day she realized how despondent I was but kept me in the snake pit regardless."

"You also mentioned being bullied by schoolchildren. That, too, can have long-term consequences on a child's development. But we'll explore those experiences as we get to them..."

As the doctor explained various effects of trauma, I nodded, recognizing many of them as applying to me, even now, all these years later. Dr. Beal's voice, compassionate and empathetic, was soothing to listen to, and I began to appreciate his experience and knowledge.

Walking home after this session, I thought about my lifelong ups and downs and bouts of depression. It all started at age four, I thought to myself. It stems back to visualizing a park with swings and asking Mum if she and I could enjoy a day together and being told no. It stems back to jumping out of a window with the idea of walking every street in sight until I found my grandparents. It stems back to the fact that as a little kid, I'd already learned attachment and, perversely, detachment. I was happy before being taken away. Totally happy. I remember it so well.

I had learned the transience of safety, home and family and the imprint remained. And so, as a teenager, I traveled to find myself. But I had to contend with a lot of shit first.

5

Four year olds are more prescient than most adults give them credit for. At that age I could often read people's moods and tried but sometimes failed to tread correctly, usually when an adult's emotions flipped without warning.

My mother could be extremely angry and strict, or she could be sweet and indulgent. One thing she had in common with her husband was a lack of patience. In the same way Terry could fly off the handle instantly, so could she. I felt I was walking on eggshells all the time and tried to behave, but sometimes I could not do what she wanted, such as when she washed my hair in the kitchen sink. I hated having my hair washed, because she was rough and scrubbed my head, unintentionally pulling chunks of hair. It hurt my scalp terribly.

I think she just wanted to get it over with, but her consistently harsh treatment put such a dread of the kitchen sink in me, that one day I felt I just couldn't go through with it when she summoned me, shampoo in hand.

She dragged me onto the chair and pushed me over to wet my head in the bowl. I howled. There I was yet again, bent over with her yanking at my hair, soapy water stinging my eyes, getting into my ears. I cried at her to stop and then Terry was at the kitchen door, yelling himself hoarse at me to shut the fuck up. I screamed with pain as my mother continued scrubbing through the noise. Terry pushed her aside, grabbed me by the ankles and hung me completely upside down into the bowl of water. I struggled, trying not to choke, as he lifted me by the legs and dunked me again head first into the water, keeping me there. I began to swallow water. Suds seeped into my nasal cavities. He lifted me up and dunked again. I began to choke and finally my mother pulled at him, telling him to stop. She grabbed me and laid me on the floor and Terry stormed off, calling me names.

After that, any time I got upset when my mother washed my hair, she'd warn me that if I didn't behave she would call Terry in to dunk me. The threat would shut me up instantly. I'd scrunch my face, grit my teeth and do my best not to show any emotion during hair washing.

No matter how volatile my mother was, though, Terry was worse, and no amount of obedience on my part deflected his intentions when she was at the office. No event is clearer in my memory than the morning I was sitting on the living room floor looking at a picture book.

Terry kneeled in front of me and told me to turn around and lean over. I did so, afraid to disobey, but thinking it unusual. If he was going to slipper me, he always preferred to wrap me over his knee. He'd never told me to stand and bend before.

As I bent, staring at the floor, I waited for the slaps to come. They didn't. Finally, I turned my head to see what he was doing. He grunted at me to close my eyes and stay still. I obeyed.

Suddenly, an internal combustion sent me shooting through the air, banging my head on the wall. I fell to the floor shrieking in agony. He was still kneeling where he was. Somehow I got to my feet. Blood gushed down my inner thighs and sank into the rug like an oil spill on sand. I screamed.

Terry dashed to the kitchen, returning with rags, and laid me on a towel to mop me with a wet flannel, then proceeded to clean the carpet. As usual I was put to bed before my mother arrived home. I don't recall him trying this again, but he inflicted many other shocks.

One day he waited until I was on the toilet and then flung the door open to stare at me like I was a laboratory rat. I told him I couldn't pee until he left, but he stood smirking. I sat still. Finally he closed the door. I began to pee and he quickly opened it again, saying, "Caught you, dirty girl," and laughed as I sat, embarrassed, on the seat.

Later he sent me into the outhouse to get something, but as soon as I went in he slammed the door and reached over the gap at the top to push the latch closed. I was trapped and screamed to get out. He said I'd have to wait until he felt like releasing me. I spent a long time, cold, sitting on the floor. He began to lock me in every day.

I became accustomed to sitting on the bare tile, staring at grime, until I figured a way to stand on a box and leap for the door, hanging onto the top where the gap was. With one hand gripping the ledge, I unlatched the bolt then dropped to the floor and let myself out. I headed out back to run off, but Terry caught me before I made it to the garden gate.

For once furious instead of fearful, I fought back, attempting to punch his face, and as he carried me in I began hurling insults at him, using the "f" word he'd screamed at me so often. Surprised, he grabbed my wrists with one large hand and, refusing to surrender, I began kicking instead. Inside, I continued to fight through the hard slaps to my head, screaming in rage as much as pain, refusing to give in until I finally tired out and lay panting on the floor. After that, Terry stopped locking me up.

Many times I heard Mummy come home from work and wanted so much to run to her, but I was always put to bed before she arrived, even though Jeanette was still up. I once heard Terry explain to my mother that because I didn't nap in the afternoon, I was tired by six o'clock, but I'm sure the real reason was he didn't want his wife knowing what he'd been doing. He needn't have worried. After his demands for silence and his threats, I was too frightened to tell her anyway.

Sometimes, though, I was still awake mid-evening when she came to check on me. He always came with her, and together they'd kneel by my bed, stroking my hair. Mummy kissed my forehead, held my hand and talked for a while, and Terry would smile lovingly and hold out a bar of chocolate. "This is a treat for

My half-sister and me. I recall being told to smile for the camera, but I see fear in my eyes.

you," he'd say gently. When he first did this, I was so surprised I didn't even reach for it.

"Come on," said Mummy. "See what Daddy's bought for you." Unable to understand why his voice and tone were suddenly so unrecognizable, I lay frozen. Then Terry looked sad and his voice trembled.

"She won't behave or respond to me, no matter how I try to please her," he said. "Now she won't even take the chocolate I've brought. I know I'm not good-looking, and she recoils from me. I can't help it if I'm ugly, but I try so hard. I wish she'd accept me."

He sniffled and Mummy looked angrily at me. "Take the bar of chocolate and say thank you." I did what I was told. "You should be grateful," she said. "Daddy tries to please you, so don't be nasty to him."

So I began accepting the chocolate. I'd wait until they'd gone downstairs and then eat the whole bar silently in the dark whilst trying to understand how he could shout and slap all day and then suddenly give me sweets. I hadn't learned yet of the term two-faced. And I was way too young to understand the concept of façade.

Terry allowed me to play with a boy and girl at a house around the corner. I suppose even at these times I'd ramble on about finding my real house and Nana and Grandad, because one day the parents were in the garden while we were playing and Mr. Smith suddenly exclaimed, "There's something wrong with that child, I tell you." I looked up and saw he was staring at me, but in a kindly fashion.

"Shh," said his wife.

"She needs help. Can't you tell?"

Mrs. Smith ushered her husband into the house. Suddenly I realized he understood. I thought about his comments for a couple of days, and one afternoon I knocked on his door. Mrs. Smith opened it.

"Can I speak to Mr. Smith?"

"What do you want with him?"

"I'd just like to talk to him."

"First, you tell me what you want!" She sounded angry.

"He said I need help. Maybe he can find my Nana and Grandad and my real home."

At this point, Mr. Smith appeared at the living room door, just as his wife turned on him and shouted, "Now see what you've done. I told you, you shouldn't have said anything, you fool."

She turned back to me. "Get away from here and don't come back. You hear? We're not busybodies, and we don't make trouble! Just leave."

I stared past her at Mr. Smith, who looked beaten. He dropped his gaze and turned his back as Mrs. Smith slammed the door in my face.

I stopped hoping for help from anyone, but to my amazement one morning my mother announced Eleanor was coming for a week's holiday. I hardly dared believe it—I hadn't seen anyone from Northingthorpe since being brought here. I vaulted into Eleanor's arms when she arrived. She'd traveled by train and bus the same as we had, for none of our family had a car. I sat by her feet that first evening as she talked to us about Northingthorpe, and she read me to sleep that night.

The next morning Terry and Jeanette and I were dressed before Eleanor woke, and my mother dashed off to her office. Eleanor finally emerged and after breakfast brought out gifts for Jeanette and me, two child-sized packs of cards. I received the blue-backed pack and Jeanette got the red ones. I happily laid mine out on the floor, remembering how I used to do this with my uncles' cards. I liked to put all the clubs in one line, all the spades in another and so on. As I was sorting them, Jeanette came over from playing with her set near her daddy's chair and began grabbing my cards. I took them off her, telling her these were mine, and Terry yelled at me to stop being mean and to give Jeanette the cards. "But these are mine," I sobbed. "She has her own. Now they'll get all mixed up." But Terry told me to be quiet and let Jeanette play.

He began telling Eleanor what a horrible kid I was, always whining about something. Eleanor watched me silently, and tears streamed down my face as Jeanette picked up all of my cards and made off with them.

The morning Eleanor was to leave, I crept to her bed and whispered to her to take me back to Nana. She quietly told me she'd talk to me later. Mummy said her goodbyes and went to work. Eleanor got packed and ready to walk to the bus stop. She cuddled Jeanette, thanked Terry for cooking, then took my hand and told me to come into the garden to say cheerio. I walked her to the gate, quietly pleading with her to take me. She crouched on her knees for a hug. I could see Terry studying us through the dark window like a lizard in the shadows.

"Sheila, I can't take you, but you'll see me again soon. I promise."

"But I want to see you now," I said. "And I need to see Nana. Let me come. We can wait till Terry's not looking."

I started to cry, but she stopped me. "She-she, please be patient. Listen to me. Things will get better. You will see me again very soon. Can you wait 'til then? You have my word. Okay?"

I sensed she was telling the truth and felt a bit better. Eleanor asked me to stay in the garden until she reached the end of the street. "At the corner, I'm going to turn around, and I want to see you giving me a big wave and a smile. Will you do that for me?"

I nodded. To this day I can see her in my mind's eye, with her fashionable updo and flared orange skirt, walking along the street with her little suitcase, then stopping to look back at me. I raised my arm and nodded. She waved and was gone. I turned. The toxic toad's eyes still gleamed from the murk as I walked back into the house. Things were still bad, but now I lived in hope. I told no one what Eleanor said, but she'd made a promise. I didn't have to feel discarded anymore. Eleanor loved me, I was sure.

* * *

I gave Dr. Beal a half-smile as he cocked his head questioningly. I'd stopped recounting my story to enjoy the memory of that hug in the garden and the quiet, loving way my aunt reassured me.

"What I didn't know until Eleanor told me years later, is that her parents sent her as a spy. She wasn't there just for a holiday; she had come to see how I really was. After all, Nana couldn't walk, and Grandad was tied up working six days a week to keep food on the table. So they'd asked Eleanor to come."

* * *

A short while after Eleanor left, I was told she was returning. She was going to take me for a two-week holiday to Northingthorpe. I scarcely dared hope it was true, and each morning I asked Mummy if this was the day Eleanor would come. I think my mother was exasperated by the time her sister finally arrived.

I rushed to the door upon Eleanor's entrance and said, "Come on, let's go!"

Eleanor laughed and unbuttoned her jacket. "She-she, I only just arrived. I'm staying overnight and then we'll go, alright?"

My disappointment must have been evident, because I recall the wounded expression on my mother's face. I didn't want to hurt her, but I so wanted to see Nana and Grandad. Eleanor got out the gifts she'd brought with her. Mine were crayons and a sketching pad this time. I set to work drawing beautiful pictures, carefully matching the colors. I drew birds, sandcastles, flowers—everything I knew Nana and Grandad liked. I spent the rest of the day drawing. At one point, kneeling on the kitchen floor sketching yet another picture while others were stacked near the wall, I heard Terry behind me.

"What's got into you? Fancy yourself an artist?"

I responded happily. "I'm making nice pictures for my Nana. They'll be presents for her!"

The next morning, I rose early, excited. Mummy said goodbye and left. I peeped out the front door, watching her walk along the street, waiting to wave when she turned. But she didn't. Perhaps she was running late. As I waited for Eleanor, Terry beckoned me into the kitchen. He pulled a chair over to the window and told me to get on it. I did so, wondering what he was doing. He ordered me to look outside. I saw smoke rising from the metal dustbin at the end of the back garden.

"It's on fire!" I said, scared.

"Yep," he said. "Take a peek into it." He opened the back door. I stood where I was. I was afraid to go near a fire, but he pushed me outside. "Go on—take a look."

I walked slowly to the can, very afraid of the smoke. Upon reaching it, I looked down like he told me. And at the bottom of the dustbin were the remains of the pictures I had spent the previous day drawing. I recognized them only from small fragments that hadn't burned.

I wanted to cry but glanced back at the house where Terry was leering at me, his eyes mere slits behind his black frames. Suddenly, and for the first time in my young life, I was determined not to show my emotions. Knowing I'd be gone soon gave me strength. I strutted back inside and smirked at him, saying, "I don't care, Terry. When I get back to Northingthorpe, I'll make Nana lots of new pictures!" I made myself laugh.

This got me thrown from the kitchen into the hallway, but Eleanor appeared and, seeing the tail end of this episode, she said she didn't need breakfast, thank you very much. She took my hand, picked up the suitcase and we left. But as soon as we turned the corner and were out of sight, I cried about the pictures.

Though I had nothing to take to Nana and Grandad, I was excited to catch the bus. When it finally came, I couldn't sit still. It was surprising Eleanor didn't go insane for I asked her repeatedly if we were near Northingthorpe yet. First it was, "No, this is only the bus; we have two trains to catch." Then it was, "No, the train ride will take a few hours." Then, "No, we need another train."

I didn't mind the wait. It was enough to know I was actually going back. Nothing could have upset me on that journey. I bounced around the bus, danced on the diesel trains, sang loudly, and must have completely exhausted Eleanor, but she didn't seem to mind.

Finally, as we pulled into Northingthorpe, I recognized the church, the park, the shops. All the way home, I bubbled and burst with excitement. I had been gone a year and now gazed with wonder at the familiar buildings, the beautiful trees, the pretty gardens.

At the bottom of Felicity Close, Eleanor said, "Let's play a trick. You hang back a bit, and I'll go in first and tell them all you couldn't come. You crawl past the window so nobody can see you, then dash in and surprise everyone."

I thought this was a grand idea, a good surprise for Nana. I could see her in my mind's eye, as I had done all this time, sitting in her armchair in the corner: balls of wool and heaps of books at her side. I envisioned her disappointed that I was not able to make it.

I waited until Eleanor walked into the house. She left the front door ajar, and I crept, guerilla-like, past the front window and quietly into the house.

I looked at the dear old stair banisters, breathed in the familiar smell of wood and pies and waited outside the living room door, hearing voices and knowing Eleanor was telling her tale. And I could refrain no longer. I had waited a long time for this.

I burst into the room and yelled, "Nana! I'm here!" And there she was. Suddenly I felt very, very tired, silently walked past my uncles and Grandad, past the old fireplace, and stood in front of her, gazing at her face. "I'm home now, Nana," I whispered.

She sobbed and held out her arms, and I climbed onto her lap, thumb in my mouth, and curled up like I used to. And suddenly I was surrounded by everyone, all stroking my hair, calling my name, hugging me.

6

Northingthorpe seemed the same but was different in intangible ways. I'd changed too. I was a distrustful five year old, nervous and often angry or miserable.

Every time I heard the front door open, I dashed to the other end of the long living room and dived under my grandparents' bed to hide. A long bedspread covered it that reached the floor, and nobody could see me underneath. Because of everybody's comings and goings, it became a frequent occurrence to see me bound through the room to the safety of the bed.

Mishaps occurred, though, such as the time I was sitting in front of a roaring fire near Nana's chair. Listening to the TV, I didn't hear activity in the hallway, so when the living room door suddenly opened I screamed, thinking Terry had come to get me. I instinctively backed away—almost falling into the fire. Nana shrieked, but, unable to come to my aid due to her almost useless legs, she wasn't able to stop my fall. Luckily I managed to collect my wits in time and twisted to grab the mantelpiece before I lost my balance. A doll I was holding fell into the fire, and the uncle who was the cause of this alarm had to quickly retrieve it. The doll was left with a permanently dented head where the fire melted it.

Nana instructed everyone to knock on the front window and wave before coming in so that I knew who it was. It was a while before I stopped being nervous about the front door and in the meantime a brass fireguard was positioned in front of the fireplace.

However, I could never quite believe I wouldn't be sent off again, and I would run away, even from Felicity Close. I had outbursts and ran out of the house and along the terrace to escape from everything.

One of my uncles would be sent after me and many were the times I could out-run him for quite a distance. The most innocent things triggered me, such as one time when Grandad reached for the poker to stoke the fire. I screamed.

"Don't tell me he even hit her with one of these." Grandad looked aghast.

I ran into the kitchen and made for the back door, but was I caught by Ed, brought back, struggling all the way, and gently placed on the rug in front of Nana. Grandad kneeled in front of me and asked me if Terry had hit me with a poker.

Sucking my thumb, I shook my head. "No, but he said he would if I got too naughty, and he used to swing it near me."

Another thing that sent me running was the threat of having my hair washed or even simply combed. It reminded me of the episodes with my mother. I'd learned to hate anyone coming near me with a brush. The association was pain and I struggled every time, no matter how gently anyone attempted it. Finally, Nana asked if I'd like my hair cut short, saying it would make styling my hair easy and painless. I readily agreed, my hair was cropped and the problem disappeared.

One problem that didn't disappear was my flashbacks. These emerged in a weirdly abstract, allegorical manner; for instance, a mountain peak kept resurfacing. Frequently, I'd be playing nearby while my grandparents watched television, everything peaceful. Suddenly I'd become aware of a hard, rocky mountain shaped like an upside down ice cream cone, pointed and sharp at the top. This peak would explode from the ground directly underneath me and rise into the air, its point catching me right between the legs, sticking into me, raising me up with it into the sky. I'd drop everything, almost feeling this mountain peak physically, then collapse, clutching myself. Grandad would carry me over to Nana's lap, and they'd stare at each other helplessly.

*   *   *

During counseling, Dr. Beal gave me insight into what he felt I'd suffered from.

"It was post-traumatic stress disorder—PTSD. An emotional illness classified as an anxiety condition. It develops due to very frightening, life-threatening or dangerous experiences. Sufferers relive traumatic incidents in some way and avoid places, people, or things that remind them of the events. This is why you reacted as you did when you returned to your old home, Sheila. Soldiers returning from battle frequently suffer the syndrome, as do survivors of natural disasters and vehicle accidents."

I waited for him to continue.

"Children who have gone through prolonged traumatic events can endure jumpiness, flashbacks, anger and many other symptoms. PTSD was officially recognized in the early 1980s. It can result in long-lasting difficulties with many facets of emotional and social functioning."

"Definitely me, then. I felt I'd been taken away because I wasn't good enough to stay with my grandparents. At age four, I believed it was my fault Terry inflicted himself on me. I was a dirty girl, and a nasty little fucker. Ever afterwards, as a kid, anytime someone showed even the slightest impatience, let alone the bullying I later experienced at school, I believed it was because I was ugly, filthy, unlikable, and I was to blame." I sighed. "I think I dissociated from myself. Sometimes, out of habit, I still catch myself doing this."

Dr. Beal looked grave. "And it's my job to help you get past it." He gave me a reassuring little smile. "Please continue."

"A few weeks after my return, I was told my mother was coming to visit for the weekend. I immediately asked if Terry was coming. The answer was yes. Nana reassured me she'd keep him away from me, for by now after patient prodding, the family had learned something of my ordeal. For weeks after I returned to Northingthorpe, Nana told me later, my little bottom was raw from continual spankings and I shook almost all the time. I sucked my thumb far more than was normal for a child of five, and I spent a lot of time hiding in various nooks and crannies in the house. I felt safer in them. As well, due to my nightmares, Grandad moved upstairs so I could sleep downstairs in the big bed with Nana.

"My grandparents were furious with Terry and also angry with my mother for allowing this to happen. How could she not have seen how affected I was, they wondered. Even if out working, surely she'd noticed Terry's aggression.

"By now they'd learned from me about the slipper beatings, but they found it difficult getting me to talk about anything else that happened to me in Manchester, at the hands of my mother or Terry.

"However, my mother by now had another baby, and perhaps that was why she was still living with her husband. What could she do, where could she go, with toddler Jeanette and baby Dana? Her parents, with several young adults still living at home, barely had the space or money to help support me, let alone two more. But now she was coming to visit and I did not wish to see her in case she was mad with me for leaving. And I definitely didn't want Terry to lay eyes on me."

"They were going to allow your stepfather into the house? After what he'd done to you?" Dr. Beal looked puzzled.

I shrugged. "When they arrived, I was sitting at the back of the living room with Nana reading to me. Mum came in first and walked over carrying the baby, which she rocked in her arms. Nana embraced her new grandchild and said how lovely little Dana was while I hid behind her, grasping her sleeve tightly. My mother tried to reach for me, but I backed away. She went quiet, retrieved her baby and walked into the kitchen.

"Terry then entered with Jeanette and sauntered over. I shivered and ducked behind Nana again, trying to bury my head under her body. I heard Nana say, "Get away from her!" and next thing I knew, he was gone too. They were in the kitchen and I stayed fastened to Nana, not letting go of her arm until eventually Eleanor took me for a walk. By the time we returned they'd left, and Nana's forearm showed a huge welt where I'd held on to her for dear life."

"Sheila, I don't understand why they let him come in. Why would they do that?"

"I think my grandparents wouldn't have allowed them to come in at all except Nana was unable to walk more than a few feet. And she did, after all, want to see her daughter and spend some time with her other grandchildren. The four of them slept somewhere else in Northingthorpe though.

"This episode made my grandparents even more aware of the need to reassure me, for they witnessed first-hand my true terror in the presence of Terry, and they saw his malevolent way of looking at me. When I was older, Grandad told me my white-faced and petrified demeanour during that visit was more than enough to make him dig in his heels when his daughter demanded my return. My mother had been led to believe Eleanor was bringing me for a two-week holiday and was told only later I wasn't being brought back."

"What effect did this visit have on you?"

"Oddly enough, the loving reassurance from my grandparents and uncles and aunt, before and during the visit, actually reinforced my sense of being loved by them all." I bit my lip. "But I felt really badly about my mother. I wanted to be as far away from her as possible, and I know she knew it. I saw her hurt look and felt awful, but I just couldn't help it."

"It's a trait I've come to know you have, Sheila," said Dr. Beal. "You are an extremely empathetic individual. It's a beautiful quality; however, in your case, it makes you blame yourself for actions you were not responsible for. It's a strong sense of guilt, akin to the survivor's guilt that some soldiers suffer from in wars. I intend to help alleviate this during our conversations."

I felt tired. Recounting events during our sessions often exhausted me. I folded my arms and leaned back as he continued.

"It's about being fair to yourself and understanding your behavior as normal. I have homework for you this week, Sheila. Go sit in a children's playground. Watch kids play on the swings. Focus on one that looks to be five years old, and think about what she'd be like if she'd gone through the horrific abuse you received."

"Okay."

"For now, we have fifteen minutes left. Tell me more about living back at Felicity Close."

*   *   *

I continued to sleep in the big bed on the ground floor with Nana. I felt safe there, and often we'd still be awake quite late after the others had gone upstairs to sleep. I'd lean on her shoulder as she watched a detective show on television, or else we'd listen to Liberace, laugh at *The Likely Lads* and hold our breath during *Danger Man*. A couple of years later saw us taking in *The Saint* and *The Outer Limits*. Nana was a night owl and it was often midnight before either of us fell asleep.

These times alone with her are one of the aspects of my childhood I recall with great fondness. To this day I can be watching an oldie on TV and suddenly remember watching the same scene with my hand gripping hers. If I had bad dreams, I'd wake to feel her arm wrapped around me tightly. These nights went a long way toward reassuring me that I was home, although I never quite believed she wouldn't change her mind and get rid of me.

There was nothing I wouldn't do for Nana, and I pestered her all the time to let me help her.

Deep down, as well, I felt if I pleased her I'd remain important to her. I didn't want her sending me anywhere again. She knew this and was distressed that I thought it. She often told me about how both she and Grandad had pleaded and even wrote letters to my mother, begging her not to uproot me. They hadn't wanted to see me go, and I found those letters decades later amongst my mother's belongings in the musty box. They reassured me—years too late— that my grandparents had indeed loved me dearly.

Soon after my mother's visit, I was once again placed in school. It was just five minutes away. Grandad walked me there and Eleanor collected me later. The first day was scary, but at least I'd been through this experience before and was resigned to a lot of kids barging around madly, bellowing and playing catch.

During the morning break I remained near the school door. I was trying to stay out of the way and noticed one girl weeping alone in the midst of the grounds. Everyone was running past, ignoring her, and she seemed lost, asking to go home. I knew what that felt like and went over, inviting her to hold my hand. Together we wandered around the flower patch until the class was called in. Still sobbing, she asked the teacher if I could sit next to her. Caroline and I became firm friends. She lived out of town. For the most part I only saw her at school, but we were good company for each other in class. We sat side-by-side, sharing crayons and helping each other to spell. During the teacher's story time, we sat together on cushions, arms entwined.

Aged 5, hair cut short

7

Slowly I began to settle into a routine at school until one day a chance remark set me back. It was near the end of class and suddenly the teacher told us we should finish our paintings quickly, because we were running late and our mummies were coming to take us home. Horrified, I dropped everything I was doing and walked up to her.

"Did you say Mummy is coming to take me home?"

"Yes," she said. "Very soon."

I went outside to see if I could hide, but the only bushes along the driveway were small and wouldn't conceal me very well. I wondered what to do. I didn't want Mummy to take me back to Terry, but where could I go?

I wandered back into the classroom, sucking my thumb as the other kids began to leave, and this is when I noticed the Wendy House in the corner. That would do. I'd live in the Wendy House from now on. Nobody would know. I'd just pop out for classes each day and return to the Wendy House every night when no one was looking. This seemed like the best solution.

The teacher went outside for a moment and I quickly crawled in and crouched low so I couldn't be seen from the little plastic window. I lay so I was able to see through a tiny gap between the house's wall and door, watching for the teacher to leave, which she did when the last child had gone. I continued to lie there, wondering why Nana was letting Mummy take me. She promised she wouldn't let her. But she allowed her to before, and once Terry had said Nana hated me and didn't want me, so maybe I'd done something wrong again. Maybe Nana didn't love me anymore and wanted to get rid of me. Sobbing, I decided to stay inside the Wendy House forever.

In my childish mind, I hadn't accounted for the fact that Eleanor was waiting for me outside. In fact, I didn't think she would be, because I'd been told Mummy was taking me home. When the teacher shut the door and walked away, Eleanor came into the classroom to find me. I saw her through the crack of the Wendy House door and lay still. Maybe she was here to take me to Mummy. Eleanor hurried around the room, checking behind the teacher's desk and in the cupboard then rushed out again, and after a while I thought it was safe to come out and stretch for a while.

I wandered around the classroom, relishing the quiet after the other kids were gone, then sat at my usual spot at the front table and sucked my thumb, trying to think what I'd done to make Nana angry. A movement made me look to the side, and I spotted Eleanor staring at me from outside the window. As soon as she saw me, she dashed around, and I knew she was coming in, so I made a beeline for the Wendy House to hide in total silence.

Again Eleanor marched up and down the room. I heard her call my name, then she went out and began rummaging in the other classroom. She returned and, with eyes darting everywhere, walked nearer to the Wendy House. I tried not to breathe, but she glanced in the little window and saw me lying there. Then her head and shoulders were inside and she shouted angrily for me to come out. I said no.

After pleading with me—and she must have been confused, because I always enjoyed our walk home—she took hold of my arms and yanked. I screamed all the way to the door and clung to the doorknob; it took her a while to break my grasp. Still I screamed as she pulled me along the long, deserted driveway.

Eleanor tried to explain that if I liked the Wendy House so much, I could play in it tomorrow, but I figured tomorrow I wouldn't be in Northingthorpe if I let her take me to Mummy. I cried and dragged my heels, and this went on for what seemed a long way. By the time we were at the end of the long driveway, Eleanor was sweating and panting, and she sank to her knees, her grip loosening, at which point I broke away to run the whole length back to the Wendy House. She had to come and start all over again.

This time she had a firmer grip, and when we'd very slowly and noisily arrived at Sycamore Road, one of my uncles, Antony, found us and picked me up. Struggling for dear life, I was carried along Felicity Close and into the house and, exhausted, I dashed for cover under the bed and stayed there, yelling angrily and kicking the bed with my feet. Antony, never one to be patient with me, was furious with my "temper tantrum" and demanded something be done about my behavior, but Nana told him he did not understand, that something must have upset me, and to stop shouting in my presence because he might scare me.

My grandparents had to wait for me to tire out before they could put the pieces together. They spent a long time explaining that although I lived with them, it was more common for children to live with mummies and daddies, and the teacher just assumed I did too. Grandad said he'd explain to the teacher and ask her not to tell me ever again that Mummy was taking me home.

The next afternoon the teacher called me over and informed me that sometimes she might tell the other children to get ready for their mummies, but I was to get ready for Eleanor. After that, I always understood. But to this day, I have not forgotten Eleanor's exhausted, bewildered face. She was only in her late teens—too young to understand what was happening.

Nor have I forgotten how hard my grandparents worked to help me relax and keep my mind on the present instead of the past. Nana tried to reassure me she loved me, always sitting with crochet work in her comfy corner armchair when I came in, or else peeling vegetables in the kitchen. Grandad was very kind, pedaling home from work or pruning in the garden, and he gave me important jobs to help him. Eleanor was affectionate, and I became attached to her almost as much as to Nana, because she was often so cheerful and funny.

This stability went a long way; however, it was never quite enough to stop me wondering if Terry might suddenly materialize, slipper in hand, to whisk me away and lock me up. In the house, I followed Nana, but when Eleanor went out I was worried she might not come back, and so I wanted to go with her.

Eleanor was friendly and outgoing, chatting to everyone and joking about anything. I loved tagging along when she went to the salon. Beehives and other updos were in fashion, and she'd sit having her hair done, laughing and talking with the stylists while I played for the whole hour with the salon's tools of the trade: big plastic hairpins and bright curlers of every shape and size, some small and hollow, others fat with metal strips and bristles, and still more with clips that snapped shut with a pleasing pop. They were purple, turquoise, deep pink, yellow, and were soft and rubbery or hard and crisp, and I was absorbed for hours, lining them up by color or else pretending they were my pets and I'd train them to sit, stand, or do tricks. I gave them little voices, and they talked to each other, played football and ran at the beach. Often I was completely engrossed in some activity with these humanized curlers and wouldn't want to leave when Eleanor was finished, but I'd obediently return the curlers to their trays, knowing they'd still be there the next time.

The year I'd spent in terror I'd withdrawn into myself, but I'd always been a dreamer. I was good at make-believe with almost any object—if it wasn't the salon's hairpins, it was sticks that became magic wands, or pieces of string that transformed into fishing rods. In order to play, I'd been forced to be imaginative with everyday things due to my serious shortage of toys since returning to Northingthorpe.

Sometime during my first month back, I'd gone upstairs to find my ottoman. Upon opening it, however, I'd found blankets and sheets instead of my toys. In a panic, I pulled them out, hoping my toys were underneath, but they were nowhere to be found. I wept uncontrollably until someone found me and carried me downstairs. I asked where my things were and was told they'd been taken to Manchester with me. Now it dawned on me that the toys I'd once played with here were the same ones I'd played with in Manchester. It meant Jeanette and Dana now had my hoops, balls and rag dolls.

My heart was broken. With the exception of Rosebud, everything else was gone! I cried a long time over my lost toys.

My family was poor and, like many others, struggled for years to bounce back after the Second World War had taken its toll on finances and jobs. No one had much money to spare, but somehow a little cash was rummaged up and Eleanor took me to a toyshop. I was made to understand that I couldn't buy much, just a couple of things, but gradually I would accumulate other toys as time went on. I chose a plastic trumpet and a bucket and spade for the beach. And Nana found some old clothes and made me a couple more rag dolls.

I soon got a few more things, thanks to the kindness of others. For instance, Grandad gardened part-time for an affluent family in another part of Northingthorpe, and periodically these people sent Grandad home with odds and ends for me. Toys discarded by their children became my exotic treasures: tin soldiers, a bow and arrow, plastic bricks, a tiny tea set and even a few dresses.

*   *   *

After the summer when I was six, my class transferred to the building at the far side of the field. This was the second year of junior school, and my group consisted of previous classmates plus new ones.

This is when the bullying started, likely because of my timid nature. I still sucked my thumb obsessively and most of the kids in this new class began to ridicule me. I tried to ignore them and spent playtimes quietly with Caroline on the outer rim of the field. One morning when the teacher briefly left the room, a boy called Stuart, who sat behind me and enjoyed swatting me with a ruler, approached with a smile.

"I want to show you something," he whispered, nodding to the small room at the back where supplies were kept. "It's in that cupboard." The teacher, Miss Shull, had left the door ajar. "Come and see," he said in a friendly voice.

Thinking he was trying to be nice for once, and wishing to respond in kind, I said "Okay" and followed him into the storage room.

"Look down in that corner." Stuart pointed to a shelf. As soon as I crouched to see, he ran out and slammed the door, leaving me in darkness. I heard other kids laughing and I banged on the door, unable to reach the handle.

"Let me out. It's dark," I cried in panic.

I heard Stuart hoot loudly. "No, we'll keep you in there forever."

I screamed and kicked the door, then collapsed to the floor, shaking. From being locked in a cupboard by Terry to being shut in this dark room by these kids, I felt my whole life consisted of forms of captivity. Now I was in the dark and Stuart said it was forever. I thought no one would ever find me and I'd die of thirst.

The door finally opened and an angry Miss Shull glared at me. "What's happening?" she demanded.

Sobbing, I told her, but instead of reprimanding Stuart, she scolded me for being stupid.

"You know you're not allowed in the cupboard anyway," she said. "You shouldn't have listened to him. You deserved what you got."

I sat back at my desk to the snickers of the other children, unable to prevent myself from bursting into tears several times during the day. After this, it was open season to prey on me. The kids simply knew they could get away with it. Following Stuart's lead, they poked their tongues out or taunted me on the playground. Often I'd come back from a bathroom break to find my schoolwork scrunched up and placed on my chair. I got no support from the teacher. Anytime I tried to talk to her, she said I should learn to stick up for myself, without explaining how one small child was supposed to take a stand against twenty others. I began to resent her for always blaming me for any wrongdoing. Between this trouble at school and my insecurities at home, I began to tune out almost everything.

*   *   *

"That woman was in the wrong vocation, I tell you!"

I had just recounted Miss Shull's apathy to Dr. Beal. "I'd love to bump into her one day, tell her who I am and then slap her smug face."

"I understand," Dr. Beal said. "Although now that I know you better, I don't really believe you'd slap her. You come across as a gentler person."

I sighed. "Right. But I'd give her a talking to, big time. She'd get screamed at if I ever saw her again. I don't care if she's elderly now. I'd yell at her. I was just a little girl and I needed protection from those kids. She didn't give it." I realized I was jabbing the air. "I was a fruit fly in a nest of spiders."

Dr. Beal smiled sympathetically and tilted his head in his customary way. I was becoming familiar with his mannerisms.

"She knew I'd gone through a tough time," I continued. "My family had told her when I joined the class, about my year's absence and about the beatings by Terry."

"Although I'm not defending her, I should remind you that no one recognized or even had a name for PTSD until 1980," Dr. Beal told me. "So in the 1960s when you returned from Manchester, medical help wasn't sought..."

"Ha. Especially where I lived in England. People were just expected to be stoic and get on with it and this included children. Pick yourself up, dust yourself off and continue."

* * *

December arrived. At school we were to paint a Christmas scene: Rudolph the Red-nosed Reindeer, Jesus in the manger, a snowman, or anything else that took our fancy. We were given crayons and paints, and as usual I sat next to Caroline, who began drawing a Christmas tree with pretty ornaments. I chose to draw Father Christmas—Santa Claus—giving presents to Caroline and me.

I sketched a red hat with a white bobble and drew him facing to the right, in outline, giving him a blue eye looking to the side. His moustache was fluffy, and the mouth underneath was smiling. A long white beard came next, followed by plump arms plus a round middle just like the jolly man should have. His arms reached out. I intended to draw pretty wrapped boxes in his hands, but first I crayoned his sleeves and jacket.

Then I found my pencil drawing something else.

At the top of his pants, about where his crotch would be, I drew a large penis emerging from his fly. Drops of fluid dripped from the end. Next I painted myself and Caroline, both with our backs to Father Christmas. Our mouths were drooping downwards, and we were running away. Lastly, I painted his hands, which were supposed to be bearing gifts. Instead they were claw-like with sharp nails reaching toward us. To my horror, I realized my Santa had changed into Terry.

Miss Shull, making the rounds, grabbed my page, yelled that I was a disgusting little horror and yanked me out of class and through the hallway. I was in big trouble. She was taking me right now to the headmistress, Mrs. Williamson, and I'd be punished severely. I didn't say a word and just let her drag me by the collar. What could I say? I knew I had painted a horrible picture, although I hadn't intended to.

Once inside the headmistress's office, Miss Shull displayed my picture and told her what a ghastly child I was. Worse, I was showing this to another little girl. I could be a bad influence on everyone. I stood in front of Mrs. Williamson. I knew her; she was Sarah Williamson's grandmother. Although Sarah and I no longer played, I occasionally saw the headmistress walking along Sycamore Road. She was silent as my teacher made her case, and she studied the portrait seriously before instructing Miss Shull to return in half an hour. With a jubilant glance in my direction, Miss Shull left me to face the music. I expected Mrs. Williamson to give me the slipper or lock me up and I stood waiting, looking at the carpet while she continued to stare at the picture.

Finally she beckoned me forward with a kindly smile. She sat on a stool in front of me and pointed to the picture. "Why did you draw Father Christmas like this?" she asked. I was silent, thumb in mouth, and continued to look away as she put several more questions to me.

I didn't respond, but she did speak quietly and sympathetically.

She made me see I was a talented painter and that Santa's head was so nice. Could I try again, she asked. Draw a new picture of Father Christmas as a kind old man? She'd like it very much if I'd try. She would have Miss Shull keep me in class during the break so I could have extra time on this project. After I had completed a new painting, I was to show it to Mrs. Williamson.

I agreed, relieved to be given a second chance. I was just so surprised Mrs. Williamson wasn't angry. She couldn't have been nicer. She did, however, place the offending sheet into her bag and I suspect now that she alerted my grandparents as to the state of my mind. Not that they didn't already know.

8

The Christmas holidays began, and I helped Eleanor as she stood on a chair to pin up decorations. The house began to resemble a circus tent, with intricately cut green, yellow and red paper streamers crisscrossing the ceiling and frilly white angels hanging by windows. Bobby and Ed dragged home a Christmas tree. It smelled of forests and earth and pine, and after we'd adorned it with shiny tinsel it stood near the living room door, reflecting in its glittery ornaments the acrobatic flames of the fireplace across the room. The family and I sat one evening roasting chestnuts by the fireplace, and Nana began talking.

"You see those tiny blue flames, darling?" She pointed to our burning coal fire, and I nodded. "Well, those are fairies in disguise, dancing and playing."

"Are they?" With saucer eyes, I stared as the turquoise and sapphire flames flickered between the bigger orange ones.

Grandad chipped in. "They're called fire-fairies," he said. "They live there all year and watch to see you're being good. If you are mostly good, they let Father Christmas know so that he brings you lots of presents."

"I'm good," I said.

"Yes, you are, darling." Nana smiled. "And it's time to write a letter to Father Christmas to tell him what you want on Christmas Day. He may not be able to bring it all, but he'll do his best. Come on, you're learning to write at school now—I'll help you make a list."

A short time later my letter was complete: a greeting to Father Christmas and hopes that his reindeer were well, followed by my wish list. "How do I send it to him?" I asked.

"The fire-fairies will help," Nana said. "What you do now is throw your letter onto the fire, and the fairies will send it to him by magic."

I tossed my sheet of paper in. "But look," I said, "it's turning black and burning. He won't be able to read it."

"Yes, he will," Bobby piped in. "All of us used to send our letters like this when we were little." Eleanor and Antony nodded, smiling at the memory. "Watch. You see that fluffy black soot at the back of the grate? See now how your letter is turning into little red sparks and clinging to the soot—that's the fire-fairies sorting the individual words of your letter. The fairies are invisible when they're working near the soot, but they change your letter from paper into something very light for transportation. Look now how the sparks are being sent up the chimney. It's your letter being forwarded to the North Pole, where Father Christmas lives."

"How it works is this," Grandad said. "All the sparks are blown in the wind to the North Pole. Once there, the elves put them together again and they turn back into your letter for Father Christmas to read."

"I bet he has your letter right now," said Nana. "This all happens very quickly by magic. Then on Christmas Eve, the reindeers pull a sleigh across the sky, landing on the roof of each house. Father Christmas will climb down our chimney with a sack of presents and leave them for us."

Delighted, I spent the next week staring affectionately at the fire, chatting to any blue flame I happened to see. I imagined the fairies were like those in my picture books, wearing dresses made of petals and hats woven from leaves, with butterfly wings behind and holding a wand. I made sure to be extra well behaved.

The night before Christmas, Grandad suggested we leave a glass of milk and a mince pie in front of the grate for Father Christmas to eat, for after all he'd get hungry on a long trip from the Pole. Because I currently slept in the downstairs bed at the back of the huge living room with Nana, I tried to stay awake, sitting up every now and then to see if Father Christmas had arrived. Nana finally told me he wouldn't come if we weren't sleeping, so I lay still with my eyes closed, listening for him instead.

Next thing I knew it was morning. When I awoke the first thing I did was jump up and look straight at the fireplace. The fire had gone out, and the glass of milk was empty. All that remained of the pie was a few crumbs, but in its place were mounds of brightly wrapped gifts. I squealed in excitement, and Nana suggested I go and wake everyone so we could all open our presents together.

I got most of what I'd asked for: books, for which I unwrapped *Noddy in Toyland* and *The Bumper Book of Animals*; games, which I found to be Snakes and Ladders, Ludo and a tiny plastic pinball machine; sweets, for which I found a Christmas stocking of chocolates. I was overjoyed to find two new dolls. Nana explained one of them had been mailed to me from Mummy along with a little note that Nana read aloud to me, saying Mummy was thinking about me on Christmas Day. There were gifts for everyone else as well. Eleanor got clothes and makeup, Grandad received a tin of Turkish Delight and Old Spice aftershave, Bobby, Ed and Antony unwrapped socks and records, and Nana opened boxes of fruit jellies, stationery and books.

Hymns were sung on television and a show about Jesus' life came on. Later, *It's a Wonderful Life* kept the family riveted in between Christmas dinner and sponge pudding. Nana told me stories about Baby Jesus, and late in the evening Ed put on records of Christmas carols. Everyone sang along to "Away in a Manger" and "Good King Wenceslas." Nana played the piano. We all went to bed very late, very stuffed, and overslept the next day. I still remember this as one of the best days of my life.

After learning of the fire fairies, I continued to wave to them for the next few years. They eventually became collectors of my baby teeth. I always put the tooth under my pillow and woke to find money in its place. One time I asked Nana what the fairies used my teeth for, and she suggested I write a note to ask them and place it under the coal bucket. This I did, and the following day there was a letter for me under the bucket, written in a mystical hand, telling me,

"We use teeth as bricks to build ivory castles." I was thrilled at finally receiving a response from the fairies to my endless chatter over the years.

Looking back now, I close my eyes and thank my family for adding such charm to my life. After the lonely, gritty backdrop and hard-as-nails life in Manchester, the fairy stories and magic they all painted for me went a long way toward giving me another perspective on life.

*   *   *

"Y'know, though, Dr. Beal, I do want to mention someone in the family who really bothered me during the rest of my childhood."

"Sure, go ahead."

"I remember nothing about my uncle Antony from the time before I was taken away. He was the youngest of the five, who were, in descending order, my mother Vivian, Bobby, Eleanor, Ed and Antony. When Vivian became my mother at age eighteen, Antony would have been ten. By the time I returned from my horrible year, he was fifteen."

"Did he physically abuse you too?"

"Oh, nothing like that. He was really nasty with me though and I always felt like crap around him. Let me explain." I straightened my long skirt and rested my hands on my lap. "To me at age five, Antony was another of the grown-ups, the only one in the family with dark hair, which he wore like Elvis. He was continually irritated by my presence. I can remember several arguments I was the cause of. One time—I was about six—Antony and Nana were watching television while I was pretending to be Tarzan swimming in a lake (the rug) and swinging from creepers (leaping onto an armchair) calling for Cheetah, my chimp. Suddenly Antony lost his temper and screamed at me to be quiet.

"I froze as Nana turned to him quickly and said, 'What's the matter with you? Stop shouting.'

'I'm sick of her,' Antony said. 'I can't hear the telly with her yapping on like this.'

"Nana told him that wasn't a reason to yell at me. She said she'd talk to me about playing in the other room when I wanted to be boisterous.

'Why do we have to put up with her?' Antony asked. 'Her mother should be looking after her, not us. She shouldn't have been born anyway.'

"Nana was angry now and firmly told him to stop saying such things. Antony stomped out. I heard the front door slam. I knew my chatter had been the cause of this, Dr. Beal, and I tried to play quietly, but now I didn't feel like playing at all and instead stared unseeingly at the television. After a while, I walked over to my grandmother.

"'Nana, are you going to send me back to Mummy?'

"She dropped her crotchet hook and took my hand. 'No, darling, you're staying with us. Take no notice of Antony, okay? Just ignore him.'

"But I couldn't ignore him. Anytime Antony glanced my way he looked like he had a bad smell under his nose. I was a hateful, ugly creature. Rejected and abandoned by the only family I knew at age four, screamed at by my mother and beaten by Terry, disliked by my teacher and sneered at by schoolchildren. I now felt I was an abomination to Antony too.

"I wished, like he did, that I had never been born."

"It's understandable you'd feel hurt when you were so young and already sensitized to negativity." Dr. Beal smiled kindly.

"I think anyone would feel hurt at such a remark." I pursed my lips, puzzled at myself. I'd just enjoyed relaying happy Christmas memories and wondered why I had suddenly gone from that to this. Well, I figured, I was here about the bad stuff, not the good stuff. May as well make good use of my time.

"You'd already been led to think your grandparents sent you away because they hated you," Dr. Beal was saying. "Now you felt a nuisance to others. That's big, for a small girl to wish she had never been born. Can you remember how that felt?"

"It felt like I shouldn't be on the planet, literally. I wanted to do everyone a favor and just go to sleep and never wake up. In fact I often used to say that as a kid. That I wanted to sleep and never, ever wake up."

"And now how do you feel about that?"

"Mad. Like telling everyone to fuck off and die."

9

I learned to read and withdrew into books. Hans Christian Anderson's *The Little Mermaid* saddened me. When walking on Northingthorpe's beach after reading it I stared tearfully at the brine as waves lashed the shore, thinking of the poor mermaid unwanted by her prince and now turned into dead sea foam.

Then there were tales from mythology. King Midas turned everything he touched into gold. This backfired when his daughter hugged him and was transformed into a cold, glistening statue, leaving Midas lonely and grief-stricken until the day he died. Persephone was abducted by Hades and taken to the underworld. I identified with her completely and wondered if my abduction to Manchester was to be a similar fate to hers and that I'd be taken away periodically, like her. The thought made me shudder. I read also of Hyacinth, who fell in love with the sun god Apollo and stood waiting for him every day, turning her head as her eyes followed his chariot across the sky. He ignored her and she eventually took root, turning into a flower.

These stories did nothing to modify my view of the world as a sad, sorry place.

The news on television was not much better. One day, sitting at Nana's feet in the mid-1960s, I noticed the TV screen full of what I thought were puppets marching along with torches and ropes in hand. The screen cut to homes burning, and these strange puppets, clad in white with pointed hoods covering the whole face except for thin slits for eyes, were jeering in a way I found scary. I asked who they were. Nana, glaring at the TV, told me it was somewhere in America and that these men were called the Ku Klux Klan.

"They go around after dark and set fire to homes of black people," she explained. "They also beat them up and even kill them."

"Why?" I asked. "And why are they dressed like that?"

"Because the KKK are bullies and cowards. They want to hurt
people for just being a different color, and they wear cloaks so no
one knows who they are. By day, they are so-called respectable cit-
izens. By night, they hide beneath their hoods and do unspeakable
evil. They are wicked!"

"So what's the reason you always tell me to be polite to grown-
ups like our neighbours and teachers, when so many adults behave
badly? Why am I supposed to do what grown-ups tell me? Who
should I really pay attention to, or even believe?"

Nana sighed. "Darling, when you're old enough you'll be able to
tell the difference between good and bad people."

"Grown-ups themselves don't seem to be able to tell the difference," I went on. "And so many of them cause the wars I see on
television. I don't see why I should trust any of them. They hurt
people in the same way kids in my school do."

A little stumped, Nana went quiet. After a while, she spoke
again.

"Darling, there will always be bad people out there. Sometimes
they're so charming they fool a lot of people. You'll need to learn
to look through the charm and to watch a person's behavior instead.
Actions speak louder than words. But, She-she, there are a lot of
good people out there too."

I'd just been learning in school about Brutus, who appeared to
be a charming friend of Julius Caesar's and who then thrust a knife
into him. I couldn't understand why people liked hurting others so
much. The world seemed to be full of them.

However, I knew Nana was right about there being good people
out there too. The headmistress Mrs. Williamson was one of them,
as were the family Grandad gardened for.

I also met good people each summer. Northingthorpe's beach
was always packed with fun-loving families from inland who came
en masse to enjoy the seaside and amusements. The trains made

it an easy trip, and tourists were the town's lifeblood. Many local people made a living by accommodating families. Holidaymakers emerged from the railway station with cases, kids and Kodaks, marched a short way to the promenade and along the sea front to their digs, passing exhausted but happy people returning to the station to go home.

The tall, grand terraces facing the sea were Bed & Breakfasts. A charming two-floor complex on the green was a large restaurant upstairs and an ice-cream shop on the ground floor next to a hall full of loudspeakers calling out numbers such as "Have you time? It's number nine" and "Legs eleven, I'm in heaven" for the bingo players, while other people preferred pinball machines, one-armed bandits and penny-falls. I often wandered around, watching players try their luck at these various games whilst from the background came an intermittent "Bingo!" from winners, interrupting the ongoing rock music, beeps of machines, and ding-a-lings of jackpots spewing out coins.

Sometimes Eleanor walked me over the green to the kiddies' paddling pool. She sunbathed while I pushed my plastic green fish around the pool. Kids from out of town included me in their games. I liked playing with these city-kids, especially because my schoolmates continued to isolate me. The only time they put up with me was when the whole class played netball for our gym lesson, during which time one group or another was forced to have me on their side for the duration.

I usually put up with the mean kids in my neighbourhood, but there were occasions when I fought back. One such time was when I rode my bicycle around the block at about age eight. Sarah Williamson and her gang were playing in the street, ignoring me as they often did. I minded my own business, teaching myself to cycle with my arms folded. Round I went, circling our block several times until suddenly I turned the Sycamore corner to find the girls standing side-by-side across the quiet street in a single line, obstructing my way, holding hands and smugly watching me through slitted eyes.

I braked and asked them to let me through. "We're not letting you pass," I was told. "Go away." I pleaded with them to let me cycle in peace. "No," they said. "This street is ours. Get lost."

Suddenly furious, I began pedaling again, steering into them at high speed, scattering them out of my way. They hurled insults as I cycled into the distance and I forced myself to laugh loudly. Still angry, I quickly looped the block and rode past again, but they didn't attempt that trick a second time. Once more I came around, making sure I was riding slowly as if really enjoying myself. One of the girls tried to push me off my bike. I leapt from it and strode toward her with my hands outstretched. There must have been something in my expression reflecting my wrath, because she quickly fled. I continued cycling. By the time I next came around, they'd decided to just ignore me again, which I was accustomed to anyway, and after a few more loops I went home. Although I'd been made an outcast again, I felt better this time, because I had fought for my rights. I felt stronger and liked myself a little more.

Nana asked me why I sometimes ignored her. I didn't know what she meant, but she finally figured it out herself. One day, kneeling on the floor playing solitaire, I looked up in time to see Eleanor bent over as Nana whispered to her. Thinking nothing of it, I continued my game as Eleanor walked to the kitchen. Then I heard a loud crash. I dropped everything and swung to the left to stare first at Nana then at the living room door. Nana behaved as if nothing was wrong and kept sewing. Puzzled, I continued playing, then a crash repeated louder than ever. I jumped to my feet, staring at the door, then turned around to face the far end of the room. Eleanor was standing by the entrance to the kitchen, silently watching me with a large tin tray in each hand.

"What are you doing?" I demanded.

"Oh, just playing," said Eleanor.

"Did you think the noise came from the other door?" Nana asked. "You looked in that direction first."

Nana wrote to my mum. She came to visit and took me to an audiologist in Middlesbrough. Tests showed profound deafness in my right ear and some loss in my left, and within a few months, still just eight years old, I was fitted for a hearing aid. I hated it and only wore it at school, where, within a week, kids were pointing at it and giggling. I withdrew further from people.

Once again I searched elsewhere for company and found it in birds flitting around our neighbourhood. I'd always enjoyed throwing our stale bread into the garden, then watching from the front window as robins and sparrows descended for their daily snack. They were adorable, with wings the color of a cup of tea and little legs the thickness of string.

I now decided to train my feathered friends and composed a special tune that I whistled when scattering their food around. At first they just seemed to listen, bemused at my attempts to "talk" as they flew by. Within a few weeks, though, they began to pay attention, flying closer and cocking their heads, waiting for me to go indoors before flying down to peck at crumbs. A few months later it was quite common for neighbours to see me walking home from school whistling as a flock of sparrows and blackbirds darted from fence to fence, from branches to eaves, following me home for their supper. I was, after all, just a short walk from school, so these were the same birds I fed at home. One older man along the street began calling me a Pied Piper.

I delighted in my newfound friends and adopted them all as pets. Nana, glad I had a new hobby, occasionally added bird food to her grocery list, telling me seeds complemented the old bread as adding proper nutrition. I had fun spreading the seeds in intricate patterns between Grandad's plants so the birds could enjoy eating their food and smelling the flowers at the same time. Soon they did not even wait for me to leave the garden before swooping to land at my feet to munch before I had emptied the bag. I felt I was finally accepted by them.

When playing by myself indoors, I'd pretend I was the Bird Princess. I had a throne in one of the trees and could fly up and sit there surrounded by my robins and blackbirds, who serenaded me with birdsong and gifted me with flowers dropped from their beaks.

I chattered constantly at my grandparents about the adventures my feathered followers and I had, from having tea with fairies in forests to joining forces with angels to fight invading aliens with magic. Nana smiled indulgently and Grandad gave me a special princess-wand he'd whittled into shape from an old branch.

One day at school, my birds appeared when I was being berated by a gang for playing on the climbing bars while no one else was using them.

"Get off them bars," yelled Penny, a girl from my class. "They ain't yours."

"Well, you aren't on them, so what's the matter?" I asked.

"Only us can climb on 'em. Yer not allowed."

"Why not?"

"'Cuz we don' like yer an' nobody likes yer, stupid cow!"

For some reason, this day I felt like answering back even though I was nervous about being surrounded by a group of about six girls. "Actually I am liked, just not by you, it seems," I said with an air of bravado.

They all sniggered. "Just who could possibly like you?" asked June, one of Penny's friends.

The truth hurt. I knew she was right, for everyone except Caroline picked on me most of the time. Caroline was not at school this day, so I could not even point to her as someone who liked me, and in desperation I looked around to the on-duty recess teacher in the distance. "Miss Wright likes me," I said. She was my current teacher and was always extremely kind and fair.

They all screamed with laughter. "Her?" yelled Penny. "She's a teacher. She don't count."

At that moment, I glanced up and saw a sparrow perched on the limb of a nearby tree. "The birds like me," I answered.

More shrieks of derision. By now, Stuart and some of the other boys were closing in to listen, as Penny demanded I prove it. "Show us the birds like yer then!"

I closed my eyes, breathed in and began whistling. Suddenly the sky was full of sparrows. They came from seemingly nowhere and swirled directly above before landing in the trees. Two of them perched for a moment on the climbing bars before flying up to join their companions in the branches. The school bell signaled the end of the break. I clambered off the bars and marched past the speechless kids and back into school.

That evening my bird pets received extra treats for their loyalty. I now realize they were more interested in any opportunity for easy food than in me, but it didn't matter. The joy they gave me in my early years outweighed their real intentions.

Grandad found me a book about birds and I devoured it with glee.

10

"The biggest irony of my childhood was the yearning I'd had to come back to Northingthorpe."

I'd been seeing Dr. Beal for three months and had settled into a pattern of recounting my life more or less chronologically. It seemed the best way to have him understand how I'd come to think and feel like I did. He waited for me to continue as I took off my jacket.

"I'd been desperate to return and when I did at age five it hadn't turned out the way I expected. I'd escaped Terry, true, but mental cruelty can be just as damaging as physical torture, and the kids in my school and on my street were relentless. For the most part, I just wanted to stay home near Nana. I still hid under her bed, sucking my thumb with my eyes closed, keeping the world out and wishing I could go to sleep and never wake up. Geez, she must have found me a clingy kid."

"Sheila, your actions were normal for a girl who'd had such harrowing experiences. There were many traumas: a form of abduction, deception by family members, physical, emotional and sexual abuse by an adult, and bullying at school."

I nodded. "By mid-childhood, I was alternating between melancholia due to isolation; anger at my mother but also guilt about leaving her; and fear of losing my Nana again. Plus I felt hatred of myself, whom I saw as a nasty little fucker. I was torn, all the time.

"When I was nearly nine, things improved when I met a girl in a garden around the corner from Sycamore Road. I was a year older, and Freda had a brother two years younger. The garden and house belonged to her grandmother and Freda and George stayed there every afternoon until their parents collected them. We never bumped into each other at school because we were in different buildings, but we became pals and I played with them in their grandmother's large back garden. It was great to finally have after-school playmates."

I smiled at the memory of Freda: short blond hair, upturned little nose. She was like a pixie.

"Occasionally Freda visited my house. She was fascinated with our little backyard full of ancient utensils rusting, unused but never discarded "just in case" by Grandad, who had not forgotten the shortages of war years. He and his whole generation had learned to never throw anything away. There was an old wringer with two enamel cylinders, one broken. We were unable to turn the stiff handle, but we loved fiddling with it. A wooden barrel was full of rainwater, and Freda helped me fill the watering can and drag it around the house to water Grandad's pansies and chrysanthemums. An old chopping table had various tools stacked on it, and we pretended to be carpenters, banging strange metal instruments onto discarded pieces of wood."

"Ah yes, those austere times," Dr. Beal said. "You know, I was born in the States. I recall my own parents recounting struggles during the worst of the dust bowl years down there. They, too, learned never to throw anything away. Anyway, Sheila, tell me what other kinds of activities you enjoyed back then."

"Playing ball with Caroline at school and adventure games with Freda in her garden made up a bit for the fact that I was without friends on weekends. Freda liked to pretend we were fairies and her brother an elf. Other times we'd play hide and seek.

"My grandmother did what she could to keep me busy on Saturdays and Sundays. I learned a lot from her. She loved writing poetry and stories, which got published by newspapers and magazines in various English-speaking countries. This way she accumulated overseas pen pals, people who wrote after being moved by her writing, much being about her family, wartime experiences and crafts such as crochet.

"To share her hobby with me, Nana recited poetry, both hers and the works of famous poets. She also taught me how to write poems. 'Best if it's about one subject,' she explained. 'You try to paint an image of a landscape or an emotion, but in words not crayons.' I wrote some clumsy rhymes and she was pleased. We worked on some together; I began by writing a first line, she wrote the second and so on. I often sat on the arm of Nana's corner chair, a notepad between us and our heads almost touching as we leaned forward, sounding each other out for ideas on poetry. She loved writing, be it in her daily diary, a letter to the editor or a limerick with me."

I turned to gaze out the office window. Two trees across the road swayed slightly and a grey squirrel hopped through the branches.

"Those hours of writing with Nana were some of the best times of my young life."

"Your mother was quite absent during your childhood then? She didn't visit often?"

"Two or three times a year."

"What was she doing? Where was she?"

"She divorced Terry. He refused to leave the rented house the welfare office paid for, so she left her younger daughters with him whilst searching for somewhere else to live, intending to return for them. Things didn't turn out well. As a poorly paid secretary, she couldn't find affordable housing for herself and two children, let alone daycare during the business week."

I looked at Dr. Beal and he nodded in understanding.

"In desperation Mum married a man from her ex-sister-in-law's neighbourhood. She knew Ben was an oddball—his clothes were always mismatched, his hair was like an upside-down bird's nest and he seldom talked to anyone—but he pursued her when she sep-arated from Terry. She agreed to marriage provided he'd allow Jea-nette and Dana into their home. However, in court Terry played the kindest, most hard-done-by husband ever to be left by his wife. He argued that the girls would be better off with him because their mother had run off.

"Mum tried to explain how abusive Terry had been to me, and

that she had left only to find another home for her children, but in the court's eyes she'd deserted the girls. She lost the custody battle and realized too late she'd sacrificed herself to another loveless marriage for nothing. As well, she was unable to make sensible choices. Instead of cutting her losses and leaving, she stayed with Ben.

"Still, there were some good outcomes to my mother's rash second marriage: Ben's gentleness and job stability. At last she had some security. And although Mum felt nothing for Ben, he loved her unconditionally. The fact that she was his wife made him happy. I doubt he'd have found anyone to marry otherwise, for his social behavior was strange, but I'll explain more about that another time."

"How did you know all this was taking place?" asked Dr. Beal.

"I didn't at the time. She told me these things when I was older and began asking."

"I see. Did she try to arrange for you to live with her, like she'd tried with her other girls?"

"Yes. After she'd settled into her new home with Ben, Mum came to visit us and announced to her parents that she now had a decent place for me. This time, however, Nana and Grandad were firm. I was not going anywhere. I'd been traumatized enough. Besides, they had reassured me I'd never be taken away again. I needed to believe that, they explained. Again, I learned about this conversation later. And I believe my grandparents made the right choice."

*   *   *

Looking back now as I write this, I realize what heartbreak my mother must have gone through when she returned to Manchester from that visit and walked into her new, secure, but empty house with Ben. She'd lost all her children one way or another, and although my revulsion at the thought of living with my mother was partly her own fault—she had been cruel to me at a time when I needed her most—I also know that in her own temperamental and moody way, she loved her children and the main reason she'd married Ben was for a home for us.

When Simon and Wanda came within a year of each other after her marriage, she finally lived the part she'd dreamed: suburban housewife with home and kids and husband with a safe job. My mother was now able to give up work and stay home with her babies, and in a house Ben had put a mortgage on. She had her own home and even a car. The only thing missing was love.

As for her other two daughters, Mum drove to visit them every weekend and usually stayed for hours to clean an unkempt house while her ex sat in his usual armchair watching television. However, the girls were being fed negative comments about her, and she was generally greeted with trepidation by them, as well as snide remarks from Terry. She was forced to stop visiting in her eighth month of pregnancy with Simon due to sickness. After her son was born she was too busy and exhausted getting up in the night for feedings. By the time she finally began visiting again, she found Jeanette and Dana, still so young themselves, would open the door and call to their father, "Daddy, there's a lady here."

Mum was fighting a losing battle to remain involved, and eventually she admitted to herself that for her own sanity she needed to stop going, because every time she returned home, she cried for hours, upsetting Simon and, eventually, her next baby, Wanda. Her mental state was becoming too fragile, and she had to stay away.

During good visits to Northingthorpe, Mum and I went to the park, where we laughed and played. Back home she studied my paintings and listened rapturously as I recited schoolbook stories of English kings. She made me feel important and interesting. We helped Nana bake pies and went to the beach to collect shells. She laughed at my childish jokes and clapped as I showed off my handstands and cartwheels. She permed Nana's hair and bought cakes.

Mum and her sister Eleanor spent hours gabbing about makeup and hairstyles and sometimes tried out a few new looks with curlers, using me as the model. If Mum came with her second husband Ben and their two small kids, we'd all head to the beach or take Nana for a drive: a real treat because Grandad didn't have a car. Nana loved these outings. Her folding wheelchair was strapped to the roof rack, and we'd find a tearoom for scones and jam.

At the opposite end of the spectrum, however, were times Mum intimidated and embarrassed me.

One such incident occurred when we went to buy me new shoes for a wedding.

"She-she, which do you like? These white pumps or the brown strappy ones?"

"The brown ones will go better with my outfit. And they're more comfy."

"Okay." She gave them to one of the two saleswomen. "We'll take these, please."

"That'll be £2/16/4d."

"What? That's way too expensive for children's shoes!"

"They're not classed as children's shoes. They're for adults."

"I asked you to show us shoes for my daughter. She's only nine years old."

"You asked for dressy shoes. Children's shoes are over there."

"But all you've got on that shelf is black school lace-ups and plastic beach sandals." Mum was beginning to raise her voice. "There are absolutely no other choices on that rack."

"Well, kids don't normally need any other kinds."

"*What?* That's ridiculous. You don't think children need shoes for weddings, things like that? What's wrong with you people in Northingthorpe shops...that's pathetic. You should *not* be charging me full price for a child."

Mum was full-out yelling now. I cringed as the two assistants folded their arms and stood stubbornly silent. "You can always go somewhere else," one of them said.

"You know damn well there are no other shoe shops in this town. I have no time to drive around other villages and towns trying to find another store. You should give me these shoes at a child's price. If they fit her, then they're for a child!"

"There are many petite women who buy them. This is the price. Firm."

Mum stomped around the shop, pointing at the tiny section of shoes for children. "Utterly disgraceful to take advantage by not having enough selection. You're coercing unsuspecting shoppers to pay more. This is fraudulent pricing of small shoes." Her face was contorted with rage. She flung the cash noisily onto the counter and grabbed the shoes. "Friggin' disgusting," she screamed. "I'll never come back here."

I sat mute on a stool and wished the ground would swallow me. After my mother had thrown the money, grabbed the bag and stormed out, I followed, hunched up, feeling the women's ice-cold eyes boring holes into my back. For a long time I crossed to the other side of the street whenever I needed to walk past that store.

I did wonder if my mother inherited her outbursts from Grandad, who had mellowed by the time I arrived on the scene, but who, my uncles and aunt told me, was extremely strict when they were kids and scolded loudly and angrily for the slightest perceived naughtiness. As small children, they trod on eggshells for fear of offending their dad—something I couldn't imagine of my doting grandfather.

As well, I sometimes wondered if Mum's moods were because of me, especially if she didn't cheer up at any time during the visit. I figured it must be because of the angst of having me at such a young age, for by now I was aware of the whole situation. I felt guilt that she'd had to put up with so much, and there was a part of me that wanted to fix it, to make things better. I knew if I hadn't been born her life would have been different.

I decided my life was going to be nothing like my mother's. Being trapped by babies and unhappy marriages was not for me. This decision was borne of one a year earlier, when I was playing with my dolls on a wet and cold afternoon. Changing my dolls' clothes, brushing their hair, and having them sit and stand and sit again, I suddenly realized I was thoroughly bored. I marched downstairs.

"Nana?"

"Yes, darling?" she asked, concentrating on a complicated piece of crochet work.

"I'm not having children when I grow up."

"What do you mean?"

"They're boring. All you do is dress them, undress them, dress them. I've been doing that with my dolls, and I'm sick of it."

"Nonsense," said Nana. "Children are very rewarding. They talk and play and laugh; they're not like dolls."

"They're not rewarding at all. Think how my mum yells when she comes to visit, and she gets annoyed every time she has to change little Simon's clothes when he gets dirty. She's always saying how only idiots have kids. Well, she's right. And I'm not going to have any."

Nana looked up now. "Your mum doesn't mean it when she says those things."

"If she didn't, then why is she always so mad every time Simon cries? Why does she always say, 'Cat in hell, never have kids,' when she changes baby Wanda's nappy and stomp about like they're driving her crazy?"

"Your mother's like that with everybody when she's in one of her moods, not just with babies," Nana replied. "I suppose I'll have to talk to her, because her behavior is obviously affecting you. But remember, children bring great happiness."

"I'm not having any and that's that," I said. "Besides, most of them end up as mean bullies and grow up to start wars. I don't like adults or children and I'll never have any."

"Please don't think like that, darling," Nana said, but I was already putting my coat on for a walk in the rain.

I soon garnered a couple more friends in the neighbourhood and became less bored. Jill Barker lived five minutes away along a small street I seldom passed. I met her whilst picking buttercups outside her gate. I now had a playmate for weekends. Energetic and witty, she thought up new games, and I was happy to follow her mad schemes. Jill had long brown pigtails and could do backward somersaults.

The other friend was a boy with black hair and big eyes fringed with the longest lashes I'd ever seen. His parents had recently moved into a house around the curve of Sycamore Road. He joined my class, and I noticed how quiet he was. We started nodding at each other when I passed his garden, him glancing at me and then looking away. After a few weeks his eye contact lingered and I detected an expression of hope. There was something quite gentle about him and I ventured over and asked where he was from. Rochester. What was his name? Daniel Gloucester. Want to play? Yes.

We began kicking ball by the old railway line, where weeds now grew through the gravel due to the government closing so many tracks in the early 1960s. It was a novelty to stroll along where the rumble and clatter of engines once bore down. The effect of the closures—infamous to this day and known as Beecham's Axe— meant weekends and summers in our seaside town became deathly quiet. Holidaymakers became a thing of the past. A trip to the beach was just not easy for them anymore.

I mourned the loss of my city friends, as I called the holiday kids. I'd been included in their games in a way I never was at school, and now they were gone. But at least I had Daniel and Jill for company on weekends.

*   *   *

I told Dr. Beal as much about life with my grandparents as I did about life at my mother's. They were, after all, a huge part of my childhood.

"When I returned to Northingthorpe at age five after my year of horror, I developed a fear of being abducted. And after weeks of waking my aunt and uncles with screams in the night, Grandad moved upstairs so I could sleep in the big bed on the ground floor with Nana. I still feel guilty about that."

Dr. Beal shifted his position and crossed his legs in the other direction. Today he wore an ivory shirt, navy tie and charcoal dress pants. It was always something staid, to me as old-fashioned as his combed-straight-back hair, but I'd realized as the months rolled by that the subdued clothing cloaked an experienced, brilliant professional who was actually making me think—really think—in new ways. "Why did you feel guilty?" he asked.

"Because it would have been normal for my grandparents to sleep together as married couples do. Instead, Nana had to put up with being woken by a kid most nights. She and Grandad missed the intimacy of married life, sleeping in each other's arms, affectionate hugs, that sort of thing. I slept in Nana's bed for years. I feel awful about that now."

"You think you're responsible for a lot of things that actually weren't your fault," Dr. Beal said. "You'd been badly traumatized by sexual and physical abuse, you suffered separation anxiety in a big way, you were scared of your mother's moods and you were being bullied. That's a lot for a young child. But tell me, how did you feel at the time when sleeping with your grandmother?"

"Oh, I loved it. I felt safe. Often we'd still be watching TV quite late after the others had gone up to sleep. We sat in bed listening to Liberace playing piano, or watching *Mister Ed* or *The Likely Lads*. A couple of years later we were taking in *The Twilight Zone* and *The Outer Limits*. *The Addams Family* was a favourite. Nana was a night owl. It was often midnight before either of us fell asleep. These times alone with her are one of the aspects of my childhood I recall with great fondness." I smiled at the memory. "To this day I can be watching an oldie and suddenly remember watching the same scene with my hand gripping hers. If I had bad dreams, I'd wake to feel her arm around me. These nights went a long way toward reassuring me I was home, although I never quite believed she wouldn't change her mind and get rid of me. But now when I remember it, I'm sorry for Grandad. He slept upstairs. I separated them."

"Perhaps it hasn't occurred to you," said Dr. Beal, "that your grandparents felt guilt-ridden themselves. They went along with your mother in deceiving you when you were four. They let you think you were going on a daytrip when in fact you were being taken away from the only home and family you'd known and thrust into into an unfamiliar situation to live with people you didn't know.

One of whom abused you sexually as well as physically."

"They didn't know about him," I replied. "They explained, when I was older, that because I wasn't their own child they felt they had no choice but to let my mother take me."

"I know that, Sheila," he said. "But think about it this way. They realized they'd made a terrible mistake in letting you go, and knew you returned a different child. Perhaps *they* had to alleviate *their* sense of guilt, by supporting you the best way they knew how. Maybe they needed to let you sleep in your grandmother's bed. They knew it helped you. That in turn helped them."

I nodded slowly. "I hadn't thought of it that way."

Dr. Beal jotted more notes. I stared blankly at pictures on his wall.

"Y'know, there was nothing I wouldn't do for Nana," I continued. "I pestered her all the time to let me help her. Deep down I felt if I was good, I'd remain important to her. I didn't want her sending me anywhere again. She knew this and was distressed I thought it. She often told me about how both she and Grandad had pleaded and even wrote letters to my mother, begging her not to uproot me. They hadn't wanted to see me go, and I found those letters decades later. They're the ones I've been telling you about, amongst my mother's belongings in that old box."

My hand shook as I brushed lint off my slacks.

"Those letters have reassured me—years too late—that my grandparents indeed loved me dearly. And I want Nana back. Even just for one hour, I want her here. I really need to talk to her...and it's too late."

11

One evening just before my tenth birthday, I lay on the rug, absorbed in watching *The Flintstones* on TV. I felt something tickle my ear and brushed it away without taking my eyes off the screen. Something then jumped onto my back.

"Shhh, go away." Then I turned to stare as a black and white puppy bounded around the room. I forgot about Wilma and Fred and screamed with delight. Bobby smiled at me from the door.

"She's yours," he said. "Her name's Joss."

I turned to Nana and Grandad, and they smiled and nodded. "Oh, Bobby," I said. "She's lovely!" I picked up the writhing, licking bundle of fluff and buried my nose into her fur. She responded by tugging my ear, and I laughed. It was love at first sight.

From then on my walks to the beach were much more joyful. Joss couldn't be a better companion when my few friends weren't available. She and I played tug-of-war with sticks and tussled in the sand. Such was the case one Saturday when I put on her collar and told everyone we were going to the beach. Joss, a mixture inheriting all the speed her various ancestors were known for, shape-shifted as sheepdog, black lab, spaniel and who knows what else, all rolled into one perky pup, and in her early days she was the fastest pooch in town.

This particular day I watched with pride as she outran all her playmates. The tide was out and half a dozen dogs including her frolicked in delight, playfully biting and barking, and raced from one end of the beach to the other. After skimming stones awhile, I whistled and Joss came dashing back, shaking souvenir droplets of seawater over me and panting dog breath gleefully into my face. We

Sheila with dog

were both in a good mood as I put on her lead and headed up to the promenade. I decided to take the long way home around the asphalt path that ran alongside the beach toward the cliffs. We zigzagged through amusement arcades and bingo halls, walked by tennis courts and were about to pass Coronation Grange when something happened that altered my life and my sense of self.

A large stand-alone building on the promenade with stained glass windows and gothic doorways, Coronation Grange was where Grandad won prizes for his roses every summer. Other events held here varied from receptions to workshops to handicrafts sales. Today, a man came bounding out of the main door toward me.

"Come on," he said. "Hurry up."

I stared in surprise. He walked back to the door, opened it, and I could hear music and see children inside. "Be quick or you'll be too late. Come on."

I was so used to obeying adults that I tied Joss to a gate and hurried in as the man held the door. On the ballroom floor were at least fifty girls my age walking in a circle. I recognized some from school. Snaking around, each with their hands on the shoulders of the girl in front, they smiled toward the stage and moved as if they were wearing ballet shoes.

"Come on, young lady, get back to it," said the man, and I must have looked confused, because he gently took my arm and led me up.

The girls broke ranks for a second to let me in and the next thing I knew, I was another segment in this caterpillar-like line-up of smiling, half-dancing kids. I'm not sure I was smiling, and I doubt I moved with anything like the grace the others did, but at this point I figured I'd be less visible if I just copied them as best I could. After a few minutes, the music stopped, the caterpillar crumbled and girls spread in all directions to sit with parents in the audience. I slunk onto a bench, bewildered.

A few grown-ups onstage were writing notes. Music began again. This time, thankfully, it was boys who were commanded forth. Around they paraded to the stirring hum of what sounded like

African drums. Again the music stopped and the onstage adults exchanged more notes, then a call went out for younger girls in the four-to-seven-year age range. Up they got and began dancing to some sort of classical music.

I began to worry about Joss. It seemed a long time that I'd left her outside, and I suddenly realized I had a perfect excuse for leaving this peculiar exercise. On the way out, I bumped into the man who was responsible for getting me into this.

"Oh, you can't leave now," he said. "The results are just coming back. Your dog's fine. I'll check on her."

I returned to the bench whilst one of the men onstage called up six of the boys and then six younger girls. "The red-haired boy with the black shorts, the blond boy with the navy bow-tie and white shirt…the long-haired girl with the pink frilly blouse…"

Now a stately woman approached the microphone to read descriptions of half-a-dozen older girls who were to step forward.

"…blonde pigtails with pink ribbons, yellow skirt…and the girl with a black pageboy-cut wearing a purple dress, yes, you dear, step up…"

Everyone clapped as each girl came forward. At the last description there was silence, and everyone turned to look around.

"I repeat, the girl with brown wavy hair, wearing a turquoise top and grey slacks…"

Someone poked me in the back. "That's you," a woman said. "Go on."

I stood up and everyone clapped. I walked to the middle of the floor to join the other five girls, wondering what we were supposed to do this time and desperately trying to think of a way out of this. Music began again. This time we were to encircle and walk around the adults who had previously been onstage. They trotted alongside us in turn, asking such questions as "What's your favorite book?" and "Which is your best subject at school?" I almost whispered my replies and my hands shook. I was relieved when we were allowed to sit down.

After this, the three groups of chosen kids, including myself, were given letters and told to return in two weeks. Finally let out, I found Joss fast asleep near the gatepost. I untied her and we walked home. I handed my envelope to Nana, who read the note and exclaimed in surprise. She called the family together. It turned out I was a runner-up in a competition for an important children's role in a parade.

"How on earth did you get this?" she asked.

The family began asking questions.

"Who were these people?"

"I don't know."

"What parade were they talking about?"

"Don't know."

"Did you catch the name of any of these judges?"

"No, I didn't."

"Sheila, really, you're so absent-minded. Why did you go in with that man anyway? We've told you never to go anywhere with strangers."

"But it was inside Coronation Grange. There was music and all sorts of people."

"Are you sure you're not dreaming all this up? Like the times you pretend to be a fairy or the Snow Queen or one of your other games?"

But the note proved I was not making anything up. The family sent Eleanor out to make inquiries, a mammoth task since nobody could read the person's signature on the letter. She didn't know who to ask and Coronation Grange was closed now the event was over, but she managed to discover the town intended to hold a harvest festival in the late summer—the first ever—and that there had been a competition to choose the Festival Princess, along with a little pageboy and girl attendant. And yes, a girl called Sheila Locke was in the running.

Knowing me as they did, my family was astounded. "Gosh," they said, "How on earth did you pull that off? You weren't even entered and we know how shy you are."

That last part was true. I'd become a shrinking violet in Northingthorpe, after years of being heckled by local kids. Had anyone in the family even known about this competition, they would not for one moment have considered entering me, because I'd never have been persuaded to go. It was only due to the unconventional and unexpected way it came about that I became involved. Eleanor accompanied me to the finals two weeks later, where again I had to dance, answer questions, and attempt a regal walk. The judging was shorter this time.

"And the winner is, Miss Sheila Locke."

Eleanor's jaw dropped, and she gazed at me, dazzled. "Go on," she said and smiled.

Aged 10

All eyes were on me as I walked to the stage. Someone put a crown on my head and a sash around my waist. There was much clapping. Cameras flashed. I was interviewed by a man with a microphone, who asked how it felt to be the very first Festival Princess of Northingthorpe.

"I'm very surprised I've won," was all I could think of.

This was a major understatement on my part but acceptable to the adults, who seemed to think I was just being modest. In fact, though, I was almost in disbelief. Me? The ugly misfit ignored at school? I glanced over at some of the girls that had lost, who had not even been runners up. Girls I recognized from other classes or from my neighbourhood. They all had normal families, two parents, siblings, friends. A couple of them were part of the cool gang at school and I'd assumed they were popular in part because they wore such gorgeous coats and shoes or because they were so pretty. How had I won the princess role over these beautiful creatures? Me, in second-hand clothes, cheap plastic sandals—the bastard kid. How was this possible?

After being seated on a "throne" with the smaller girl and boy—my attendants—there was one last camera flash and I was released.

"Remember," called one of the judges. "You need a white dress for the parade. We'll be in touch with more information."

When the photograph of me appeared in the local paper, my 2nd-year primary teacher brought the clipping into class and posted it on the corkboard. The pupils gathered around, agape, and stared at me in sullen silence. Suspicious girls asked me how I'd managed it and what I intended to wear. Well aware of their narrowed eyes and resentment, I shrugged and walked away. I really didn't want to talk to them. The boys couldn't care less about my role in the festival and taunted me as usual. But something in me, just a tiny fraction, changed. I realized that if I'd been chosen from so many others to be a princess in a procession, then I couldn't be as horrible as I thought. As I'd been led to believe. As they saw me. And suddenly I asked myself: Why do they see me like that? The judges didn't.

The following weekend, Grandad and I waited at our usual time in the telephone box at the street corner for my mother to call. We did this each second Saturday. I wasn't sure if she'd drive over for the weekend I'd be in the festival. There were so many events she'd never made it for that I decided not to ask. I didn't want to be disappointed. I crouched and hugged Joss, suddenly realizing that if I hadn't taken her to the beach that day, I'd never have ended up being the princess.

Grandad picked up on the first ring and right away handed the receiver to me. "Tell her your news," he said, smiling.

So I told Mum about winning and to my delight she told me she was overjoyed and that she wouldn't miss it for the world. She and Ben and the kids were definitely coming, camera in hand, to see me as the town's princess. I was pleasantly surprised. Suddenly I felt more enthusiastic about the festival. Along with the rest of the family, my mother would be there.

This same summer, Bobby finalized his wedding plans.

All the Lockes liked his fiancée Grace. She arranged my gown fitting for their wedding and instructed me on my duties for their special day. I saved my pocket money to buy them a wedding present even though Nana said it wasn't expected. I wanted my Bobby, who had given me so many rides on his bike and who had found me my beautiful dog, to have a present especially from me. I chose a pretty salt-and-pepper set. Sometimes after their marriage I walked to their house after school to visit, impromptu, and Grace always made a point of bringing out the salt-and-pepper set—"One of my favorite wedding presents!" —and served homemade pie or egg and chips.

We all decided my bridesmaid gown should also be my Festival Princess outfit, for it was a creamy satin with lace detail, designed by Grace and very pretty on my ten-year-old frame.

I can see the pageant in my mind's eye even now, with Nana being pushed along in the wheelchair she seldom used. She rarely wanted to leave the house due to the difficulty of getting her cumbersome three-wheeler "outdoors" wheelchair down our bumpy terrace, but she was not going to miss this. Mum and Ben stood smiling with my grandparents on the street corner, and my uncles and aunt cheered as I was driven past. Joss spotted me and began barking, tail wagging and ears standing to attention.

The float was decked with flowers. I sat on a beribboned throne flanked by my little attendants. We were somewhere in the middle of the procession, preceded by the Northingthorpe Lions, who were dressed as, yes, lions. A truck full of mermaids and a man dressed as Neptune holding a trident followed us. Part of my function was to present prizes for the sandcastles at the beach and to judge a costume competition. I'd been given a role, and I took it seriously, playing the part as best I could. I felt that for once, my family could be proud of me. I looked pretty. I was a princess, at least until midnight.

12

Now that my mother had settled into a relatively normal life in Manchester, she and Ben drove over during the summer holidays to take my dog and me home with them for a fortnight. I was old enough now to understand that I didn't need to worry about Terry ever again.

The first few summers Nana came too—quite a feat, because her enforced sedentary life had made her quite plump, or cuddly as I saw it. Initial groundwork was needed to ensure there'd be cafeterias along the way with ramps for her folding wheelchair, and accessible bathrooms. It became a habit to stop on the way back and forth in a pretty Pennine village at the same little café that always smelled of fresh-baked scones. The owners bred dogs too, and we'd sit at a window table overlooking a large garden with anywhere from two to a dozen barking hounds larking around outside while we ate sandwiches and sipped tea from dainty hand-painted teacups.

At Mum and Ben's house, more effort was needed to help Nana through the door. The front step was difficult for her and going upstairs was not an option. She and I slept in the front room downstairs.

Mum was always overjoyed to have us. During these holidays her bad moods were generally rare. She was bubbly and full of fun ideas for days out. I found her new husband relaxing to be around, even if hard to read. He was quiet and a bit different somehow. However, before our first visit to their Manchester home, Nana had a talk with me.

"You've met Ben on a few occasions now, She-she, when he brings your Mum to visit," she said. "Do you think he's alright?"

"Oh, yes," I said. "He seems nice."

"You know, darling, you could be really kind to him. Would you like to make him happy?"

"How?"

"By calling him Daddy instead of Ben. No, don't pull a face, I know you don't like the idea of any daddy after the other one, but Ben is your Mummy's husband now, and that baby is your little brother. Ben is a good person. Could you start calling him Daddy?"

"But why should it matter? What difference does it make? I'm used to saying Ben now. I'd feel silly suddenly naming him Dad and besides, he's not my dad, is he! So what's the point?"

"Well, he might feel included and more like a part of our family."

"But I'd feel daft just suddenly saying 'Hi Dad' when I've never..."

"I tell you what, then," Nana said. "How about you talk to him about it. You could explain you're comfortable with him and think the time is right to call him Dad. I know you're such a caring person and like to be nice to people. Just think how pleased he'd be. He'd feel accepted by you."

"I don't think I've done anything to make him feel unaccepted! But if you think it's right, then I'll talk to him."

"Darling, that's wonderful. He'll be glad and so will your Mum."

So on their next visit, I explained to Ben that I wanted him to be part of the family and from now on I'd call him "Dad" and hoped he'd be happy. He twitched his face a little as was his habit, and blinked in the way he always did when he was about to say something, which was not very often. "Hmm, yes," he finally said and nodded. I stood, waiting for further comments, but although he glanced at me benevolently, nothing else was forthcoming. Soon he forgot I was there, lapsing back into his own world. I recognized this trait because it was something I often did myself—not intentionally ignoring anyone, but just off dreaming about something else. I wandered away feeling fine with the agreement, but later heard Nana ask Mum if she could get Ben to be a little more conversational with me.

Mum laughed. "When I figure out how to get anything more than a one-liner from Ben, then I'll begin working on him for others. He's just a quiet fella, okay?"

My future interactions with Dad showed me that although he had some strange quirks, he was a gentle man, good with his children, and helpful to me during visits when he realized I had trouble with math. As long as I went to him with a specific problem he'd open up and spend hours, if necessary, explaining arithmetic or some other subject. Most of what he said went over my head, but at least he tried. Years later, when I was in my teens with a motorbike, he'd drop what he was doing to assist with mechanical problems.

Dad adored my mother and did everything in his power to please her. There were, however, many things my second stepfather could not do, including changing his basic personality. He and my mother remained complete opposites. Where she exerted an outgoing energy, he remained reserved. Where she shone with confidence, he stood socially awkward, alienating himself from strangers with embarrassing gaffes and even sarcastic remarks that were meant to make people laugh. My mother became exasperated and often stormed around the house yelling angrily at him, at which times he sat quietly until she'd calmed down. Then again, Mum never, ever learned patience and also scolded little Simon and later baby Wanda anytime they made a mess.

"Oh, fuck, not again," she shouted as her six-month-old daughter wet her nappy. "I just changed you. Can't you wait at least an hour before you go again? Dammit." She snatched Wanda from the carpet, yanked the nappy off and began draping her in a dry one. "Sheila, put this in the bucket." Picking up the wet item with two fingers, I carried it upstairs to the nappy bucket, while she continued to dress Wanda with great impatience.

By the time I'd returned, twenty-month-old Simon had thrown up onto his tee-shirt and the carpet. "Jesus Kehrist, it never ends. My whole life is spent washing their clothes. You dirty little sod!"

With that, she pulled the tee-shirt off and sent me back upstairs for a facecloth and clean shirt while she scrubbed the carpet. I could hear her all the way up the stairs.

"You get dirty all the time! All the time! Fuck, only idiots have kids. Never have kids. They consume you, just consume you."

I'd take Joss outside and throw a ball for her until Mum was quiet, all the while horrified that babies had ruined her life.

When Nana came during those first few trips, she'd calm my mother down, saying how normal it was for toddlers to be messy but that they grow out of it quickly. She took over much of the nappy-changing and feeding during our stays, enjoying the time with her two small grandchildren. Dad would then take over, taking his son and daughter into the garden, giving his wife some quiet time for herself.

To her credit, Mum kept a very clean house and catered to my half-siblings' every need. It's just that she sometimes did it so resentfully. She made up for this at other times by being extraordinarily affectionate and those were the times we relaxed and were happy around her. Her second husband wasn't good at keeping either himself or the house tidy, and often walked around with hair unbrushed and leaving ashtrays full, but he did spend a lot of time caring for his children. When finished working his shifts, he read to them and threw balls.

Nana accompanied me on these holidays until I was twelve. I suspect part of the reason was to ease me into feeling comfortable around my temperamental mother and her new husband.

After a day or so of settling into the Manchester home, we walked to the shops, Mum pushing Nana, who had toddler Simon in her lap, me pushing Wanda in the baby pram. Joss trotted along beside us, sniffing every new street corner like a doggie detective. When Dad wasn't at work, we drove to Bellevue Zoo or Blackpool. Such places were awesome for a small-town girl like me. I'd never been to a proper amusement park until these holidays at my mother's. Northingthorpe's seaside boat-swings and Blue Giant Slide paled in comparison to these huge rides.

"Yippee! Come on, She-she, let's try Noah's Ark," Mum said. She was almost jumping with excitement herself, and we left Nana and the babies in Dad's care.

"Wow, it's a ship," I said, "and the deck is rocking."

"Take my hand," Mum smiled. "Let's see what's inside."

We walked the gangplank and through a curtained door at the side of the huge boat. It immediately grew dark. Small lights inside gave off an eerie glow. Mum walked through the narrow corridor in front of me, and suddenly a blast of wind blew from beneath us, blowing our skirts up.

"Eek," yelled Mum as she yanked her dress back down. I giggled. A massive animal head leaned out and groaned.

"Argh!" my mother screamed. We both fell to giggling. "You'd better go first," she said. I did so, and almost immediately the floor beneath me pretended to give way. I shrieked. Mum burst out laughing again and tried to avoid the falling-floor joke by jumping across it, only to land on another trick step that lit a ghostly crevice with a skull that began wailing. "Ooh, help!" Mum squealed and dashed around the corner as I followed, chuckling.

After the surprises of Noah's Ark, we rode bumper cars, which Mum and I charged at each other, and sat on merry-go-rounds that made us dizzy. I liked Mum joining me on these rides. At these times she was more a big kid than a mother, and we began to truly laugh together.

After fun days like this, Nana sometimes stayed home with Simon and Wanda whilst Mum and I went for groceries. This meant walking along a busy street and the first time we did this, I grew alarmed by prolonged beeps of vehicles and gazes of the men driving them.

"Mummy, why are they beeping at us? We're not jaywalking." I clutched her hand fearfully as one man drove by whistling at her.

Mum was not bothered at all. "Oh, don't worry," she said, smiling. "They're just showing their appreciation."

Another man leaned out of his window, yelling "Hi gorgeous" with his eyes locked on her as he swerved past. Although Mum didn't respond to his or any other's cries of ecstasy, I could tell she loved being noticed. She laughed in amusement and waved them off with a wide smile. The more hoots she got, the taller she walked, and I realized she thrived on the attention. But their expressions reflected the look I'd learned to dread on Terry's face when I was four and my hands tightened into fists. I itched to pick up a pebble and throw it after their cars.

After our visits with my mother, Nana and I were dropped off at my uncle Ed's place, forty-five minutes' drive away. Ed was now married with a baby daughter and we piled into their little place in Leyland and had tea before Mum and Dad went home. I enjoyed my weeks here, too, and Joss was in heaven. There was so much for her and me to explore.

The small rented house was part of a rundown, unused farm, and everywhere there were mysterious crumbling brick buildings. Joss chased mice. I found doors that opened onto steps leading deep into dark cellars, which I fantasized were host to vampire coffins. I never ventured farther than a few steps before dashing back and slamming the door shut, my heart pounding. A large barn housed sparrows fluttering in the rafters and maybe escaped convicts in striped prison outfits hid under the straw bales. The greenhouse was full of overgrown vegetable plants that perhaps turned into killer tomatoes or the pods of bodysnatchers at midnight. A coop provided fresh eggs, and I wondered if the ugly duckling had been picked on or pecked on by the resident hens. My life was still a dream world, even here.

On one such visit, I met Ed's neighbours in a house along the lane. They had a boy and girl who became summer friends. They played with me on the old farm and were as fascinated as I with the dusty skeletons of machinery. We clambered onto rusty tractors, pulled on heavy, creaking mowers, made mud pies and weighed them on a pair of antique scales. Soon we ventured farther. Government offices and grounds were nearby and the three of us pretended to be Jane Bond, James Bond and June Bond, secret agents sent as spies. We peered into office windows. Typists looked up and waved and we ducked down, out of sight of the enemy.

Whenever these new friends weren't available I had Joss to throw sticks for, or I played alone as a good witch living in an ancient mansion—one of the old storehouses—and my companions were doves, stray cats and rabbits. I conversed with them in my mind and organized them into teams to save the world. Secret messages were left for my animal friends via coded symbols written into the earth or magic stones strewn around the farm. At other times I was an Indian sage with a feather and spoke in a bass monotone, intoning spells to save my family from malevolent ghosts.

Often I was still deep in my fantasy world when I sauntered in, chanting, for dinner. Ed scolded me for being such a dreamer.

"Really, Sheila," he said. "You have one foot in this world and your other foot somewhere else."

He was right. In my dreams I was the hero, the beloved wise-woman. Why would I not want to stay in that world instead of returning to this one to be bullied by swarms of schoolchildren? Their taunts rang in my ears even here, miles away on the farm. *Hey Deaf-Lugs, where ya goin'? Where's yer Daddy, Bastard? Ew, you're so ugly.*

After the holidays with Mum and Uncle Ed, we'd return to Northingthorpe where I'd fall back into playing with my little collection of friends. Daniel and I became chummier. Jill was always the same, energetic and funny. She reminded me of a young Lucille Ball. I still played with Freda and her brother in their grandmother's garden. These activities were my break from feeling lonely in a crowd at school.

Freda and I started swimming in a nearby town that had a pool. A bus was organized to take Northingthorpe children there and Freda's grandmother accompanied us. After some months, competitions were organized and Freda and I signed up for the breaststroke, but no one from home could come to cheer me on. Nana was physically unable, my uncles and aunt were busy with their own families, and Grandad was working, so as usual I tagged along with Freda and her grandmother.

I won the race. With crummy marks at school and a loser with other kids, it meant a lot to have won a prize cup. That is, until I walked back to the changing rooms and bumped into Freda's grandmother. She shoved past me saying not a word. On the bus home, she and Freda sat together near the back, not even looking at me, let alone asking to see the trophy.

Nana couldn't understand why I presented her with my cup and announced I was quitting swimming. However, I'd decided that if winning things meant I lost friends, then there was no joy in it. Nobody had been there rooting for me. There was no joy in that either. I would not let this happen again.

I didn't visit Freda to play after that. In fact, it was she who appeared one day as I was reading in the front garden. She stood silently watching until I felt myself being stared at. I looked up and nodded, and she asked if I wanted to play. I said, "Okay." We played, but I didn't feel the same anymore. It was the end of our friendship.

13

At age ten and a half my home haven came crashing down.

Eleanor had gotten married. Her husband worked away from home, so Eleanor continued to live with us in Felicity Close. She became pregnant quickly, but her husband rarely came to visit. Eleanor filed for divorce within a couple of years, but by now she had a son. Unfortunately, I was not prepared for this new, permanent inhabitant of the house and things didn't go well.

I was out the afternoon Eleanor came home with the new baby, and when I burst in, chattering about a horn Jill had lent to me and blowing on it for everyone to hear, Nana yelled, "*Be quiet!*"

I was stunned. Nana always wanted to hear about my outings. She'd never raised her voice to me. Not ever. She looked angry with me for the first time, and I suddenly wondered if she'd changed her mind about keeping me, as she had when I was younger. Maybe she would send me away again. She pointed to the other end of the room, where Eleanor was sitting with a carrycot by her side.

"You'll wake little Dean!" she shouted. "Stop bringing noisy toys into the house!"

"Why be mad with me...I only wanted to…"

"I don't care," she said, glaring at me before returning her attention to her crochet work. "Be quiet in the house from now on."

Her new attitude was a huge blow. My life had revolved around Nana. I idolized her, and suddenly she didn't want to listen to me. I was instantly reminded of living with my mother at age four. Both she and Terry had doted on two-year-old Jeanette, putting me second the whole time.

I walked back out of the house in tears and went to the beach, my mind numb. That one episode made me realize everything at home had changed with the arrival of this newcomer. Nana had shouted at me for the first time ever. How were things to progress from here? She obviously preferred this baby to me, just like my mother had preferred Jeanette. I was going to be replaced. I stared at the waves for a long time. I was unimportant and useless. Nana no longer needed me.

Deeply hurt and resentful, I eventually returned home. I could tell Eleanor was upset I showed no interest in looking at her child. Nana said she was shocked at my meanness. This only resulted in driving me further away. Living with discrimination all my life at school and from relatives such as Antony, watching my Nana desert me in favor of another child was too much.

Had she gently asked me to lay off the horn, then shown at least some interest in what I'd wanted to tell her, then perhaps I wouldn't have felt an instant rebuff that first day. Maybe I could have accepted modifications to the family dynamic. But the fear of rejection, and haunting thoughts Nana and Grandad hadn't wanted me, surged up, and I was suddenly lonelier than ever.

I began to mentally withdraw. I felt betrayed and, in fact, was never reassured my feelings were mistaken. I was forced to watch them dote on Eleanor's child ever afterwards while only half-listening to anything I said.

Antony, now twenty, began dating Tabatha. She was in her mid-teens and I was only ten, but we talked for hours. Antony's sarcasm stopped when he realized his girlfriend and I got on so well, although I felt he only tolerated me for her sake. The pursing of his lips was a dead giveaway. Tabatha was very pretty with olive skin, a heart-shaped face and long, dark hair. I grew my hair for the first time since being small, because I wanted to be like her. She found me interesting. This was a huge boost to my shattered ego.

On top of everything going on at home, the primary school's "11-plus" exams were looming. These determined our secondary education. Daniel and Jill took the exam the same time as I did. I didn't pass, which meant I'd attend the local secondary school after the holidays, along with Daniel and many others. Jill was accepted and would start at the out-of-town, prestigious school. We all shrugged and carried on with our lives. I continued to spend time with Caroline in class and play with Daniel or Jill afterwards.

Summer holidays came and went. My mother bought my new grey school uniform then returned to Manchester. I found myself in the hectic swirl of Northingthorpe's school for older kids. We were given a lot of homework assignments, which I was not accustomed to, with a turnaround of two days. Also, I was dealing with my private terror of new kids from surrounding villages, as well as the usual ruffians.

When things settled, I knocked on the Barkers' door. Mrs. Barker said Jill wasn't in. Suddenly it seemed as if she was never in. A couple of months passed this way before I spotted her in her new bottle-green uniform. She was walking to the shops with a friend in the same outfit. I ran up behind them, tugging at Joss on her leash.

"Hi Jill," I called.

She and the other girl glanced around, then kept going. I followed.

"How do you like your new school?" I ventured.

Jill whispered to her friend, then turned and said school was fine and walked on.

Puzzled, I continued. "When can we get together?"

Again Jill whispered to her friend, who turned around and snapped, "Can't you see we want to be alone?"

"But why?" I asked.

Jill spun round. "I'm in a new school. I passed my 11-plus. You're just a dunce. Go away!"

I stopped dead in my tracks. I watched them all the way down the street until they turned a corner. Jill never turned back.

Joss whined. I looked down to see her sitting patiently by my side. She picked up a paw and tapped my knee. I hugged her, watching her tail wag as I stroked her ears. She licked my wet face. "Well, Joss," I said. "I've still got you, eh? I've still got you. C'mon, let's go to the beach."

*   *   *

I knew I was pouring out a lot of random events very quickly, but Dr. Beal wasn't fazed. In fact, he nodded as if my current state of mind made sense.

"Sorry I'm going on and on without rhyme nor reason," I said.

"Actually, there's a pattern. Here you were, in a short period of time, without anyone cheering you on during your first swimming competition, shunned by Freda's grandmother for winning it, shouted at and no longer listened to by your beloved Nana, and humiliated and dropped by one of your long-term playmates. As well, after being the only child and primary focus for your grandparents for many years, you suddenly needed to adjust without real warning to a new child in the house."

"Other kids were used to living with brothers and sisters," I said. "But I couldn't handle having Eleanor's baby in the house. It was as if I suddenly didn't exist. It was the beginning of the end of Nana and me being close. Suddenly she had no patience and it hurt horribly."

"When you first started coming here, you told me you were furious about a lot of things. These certainly have to be some of them. Whether or not you were only imagining that your grandparents had lost interest in you..."

"I was not imagining it! Wait and see. I know it's nearly the end of our hour today, but you'll see...in future meetings, I'll tell you. I lost my grandparents to that kid. And I hated him for it. I don't think you believe me right now, but wait til I tell you..."

I grabbed my bag and stood up, knowing my face was twisting into something ugly. I felt a pneumonic drill banging under my ribs. Fuck! After all these years, these memories still managed to do this to me.

Dr. Beal stared earnestly at me. "Sheila, what you're talking about is very important. You're letting it out. As well, it helps me understand more of the situation and how to approach it. You were hurt many times in your younger life, and from what you said in our initial meetings, you've been hurt in your adult life too. You say you feel guilty for being angry? I'm actually surprised you're not more angry."

"Yes, I'm mad, pissed off, bloody furious, but I want to get rid of it. I want this to go away. I feel so guilty. I'm tired...just so tired...." My voice dwindled and I looked at the floor.

"You are not guilty of anything. Your responses to treatment meted out to you is normal, Sheila. And as you once told me, these things didn't cause you to go into crime, to take revenge, what-have-you. You're not the bad person you appear to believe you are. In fact, I have found you to be very polite, kind, intelligent and sharp. And no, before you say it—I am not paid to say that!" He grinned. I smiled back, faintly, and took my leave.

14

"Sheila," Mum began, on one of her visits to Northingthorpe, "you're twelve and haven't met your biological father yet. We've arranged to meet up next weekend."

"What? No, I don't want to."

"Why not?" Mum looked puzzled.

"Just don't, that's all."

"But, She-she, haven't you ever wondered what your father's like? I thought you'd be curious." Mum pushed her blond hair back and smiled. "He and I kept in touch all this time, even though we don't see each other. You know that. I told you we send Christmas cards to each other. It's arranged and he's looking forward to meeting you."

"No! Anyway, you told me he and his wife have six kids of their own. Why would he want to see me? I don't want to go."

"What's the matter, darling?" Nana asked. "There must be some reason you feel like this."

I sighed. The continually demeaning remarks of kids at school and in the street had successfully destroyed the tiny amount of self-esteem I'd acquired by being the festival princess a couple of years earlier. I felt my biological father would be disappointed at the pathetic wimp that appeared. I mumbled about him maybe expecting a better kid than me.

"Don't be silly," said Mum. "You're lovely, and he'll be delighted."

My mother refused to cancel, and so the next Sunday we got dressed up and drove to a pre-arranged country lane where his huge car waited. Parking behind it, we walked to his vehicle. He opened the front passenger door from the inside and I bent down to get in, looking at him nervously as I did so. Mum clambered in after me, for there was plenty of room on the long bench seat. I was surprised at his horseshoe baldness for I'd always imagined a father with thick brown hair. With a hint of a smile, he took my hands in his, telling me he'd looked forward to meeting me. I couldn't think of a single response. I sat sandwiched between my mother and father for the first time in my life at the age of twelve, whilst he explained that although he'd seen me previously from afar, he'd never had the chance to talk.

Mum explained. "Sheila, you know those letters you used to write to Father Christmas? Some of those toys on your wish list were just not affordable for me or for anyone in Northingthorpe. Spencer asked me, after you were born, to let him know what to get you every Christmas. That's why you always received one wrapped super toy with no tag to say who it was from."

"I was always told it was from Father Christmas himself, which I believed for ages," I said, smiling shyly. I turned to my father. "So it was you? The Spyrograph? The pogo stick?"

He nodded, and suddenly I realized where I got my grey eyes, straight nose and small mouth.

"It was my one chance each year to catch a glimpse of you," he replied. "I drove over with the gift and your grandfather let me come as far as the living room door to see you. You'd be playing or watching television, and I saw you grow up that way, for a few seconds each December. I couldn't get to know you other than that, being married as you've heard, and with a family in Middlesbrough. I couldn't risk my reputation at work or any embarrassment for my wife, by being seen by anyone who may know me. This is why we're meeting here, in this quiet lane." He sighed. "You've been told the story of how you came to be. I'm sorry it's like this, but you know how people talk."

I nodded. I didn't know what else to say. I knew my father had remained married to his wife, who was pregnant with their third child when he discovered he was about to have another with his lover. I knew I had a half-sister somewhere only three months older than I, and suddenly felt quite sad. I didn't know anything about her or indeed about any of them.

"What do you enjoy doing? Your Mum tells me you read a lot."

"I like books about animals. And science fiction and horror stories."

"We like watching Dracula films, don't we?" Mum said. "Tell him about that Christopher Lee film we watched a few months ago."

We chatted for an hour, then it was time for him to go.

"I've brought something for you to remember me by," Spencer said and handed me a little box. I opened it to find a newly minted silver sovereign. "I enjoyed this visit and am glad we finally got to meet. I know you're in good hands with your mother, here, and living in Northingthorpe with your grandparents. They're lovely people."

He pinched my cheek gently.

"Sheila," said Mum, "go back to our car. I'll be there shortly. We just have a couple things to discuss."

From our vehicle, parked a few yards behind, I could see the silhouette of my mother and father talking, then they leaned toward each other. A lingering kiss ensued, then my mother came back and we drove home. She was silent and a little teary. I was quiet and a bit numb. The only father figures I had were Grandad, mellow and kind but often out working, and Ben, whom I called Dad after Nana asked me to. But no real father, not one to play hockey with or to take me on zoo trips or boat rides.

*   *   *

Some months after I began secondary school, Grandad became head of maintenance for the same school. Due to his being on call, he was required to live in the house that came with the job, so we all moved to the other end of town to a tiny home close to the school.

It wasn't difficult for me to leave Felicity Close. So much had changed anyway, and not only with former playmates. A year previously, there had been loud crashes and drilling at the end of my street. I found a group of neighbours and kids leaning on the wooden fence I used to sit on years earlier to wave at trains. Ahead, on the railway land, a huge ball-and-chain was smashing the side of the tall, red-brick railway watchtower. For years a many-spoked windmill had spun around like a bicycle wheel on top of this tower. I'd always found it hypnotic, peaceful to watch; after all, there was nothing else to amuse me about the old station now that the trains were gone.

Seeing the structure being destroyed was distressing, and I didn't get why everyone was chattering excitedly. Couldn't they understand it was all we had left? I asked some grown-ups to tell the workers to stop, but they told me not to be silly. After staring at the increasingly damaged tower a while longer, I walked home in tears.

So, although moving to a new house felt strange, it removed me from the pain of watching further dismantling of the railway buildings I'd grown so fond of. I was also glad I wouldn't have to deal with Sarah Williamson's gang anymore. I'd lost touch with my old friends, except for bumping into Daniel in an occasional joint class at the new school. By now, he and I were in the awkward throes of adolescence, and he'd become distant. I imagined he didn't want to be seen with me in case other pupils accused us of dating, or maybe he realized I was not cool to be seen with. The interesting conversations we used to have dried up. Eventually he found a couple of new pals and, thankfully, so did I.

The new school was as bad as the old one where bullies were concerned because they moved there with me, plus now I also had to contend with their older siblings who joined in the baiting.

I was constantly terrified of what kids might do. By now I'd come to expect to be treated as a pariah. I retreated further into my private world, which, as a puberty-driven teen, consisted of wild escapades with Captain James T. Kirk of the Starship Enterprise. I was always a beautiful, angst-ridden woman the Captain rescued from aliens and carried in his arms to the ship. He allowed me to reside in his bedroom while he slept on the couch, until, unable to contain himself any longer, he slipped into bed one night to teach me what life could be about.

I took to spending a lot of time upstairs, preening. I read the *Jackie* magazine for teenagers, articles about makeup, pop bands and what to do to attract boys; that last part, I knew, would be hopeless in my case. I separated after-school life from school life, the latter consisting of red tie and grey skirt and cool teenagers of both sexes whom I resembled not at all. For instance, a girl in my class called Jane had grown enormous breasts, and her parents could afford to buy her camel-colored suede lace-up boots that were very sexy. She was surrounded by boys, girls and, surreptitiously, male teachers. I, on the other hand, wore plastic black boots and grew average breasts. I still had my braided hair from primary school. To remain invisible from aggressive teenagers, I kept my usual hairdo. Any big change and I'd likely be noticed and taunted even more.

After school I usually scurried home, grabbed my field-hockey stick and practiced by myself in the park. If I saw a group of teenagers, I crossed the street. Sometimes Nana would have an errand for me, and I'd sigh and snatch the shopping list silently. Things were not going well at home. The maintenance manager's cottage was tiny and claustrophobic. By now, everyone had married and gone except Eleanor, who was finalizing her divorce. She was often cranky. Nana and I didn't talk much anymore, Grandad silently watched television, and I sulked and spent a lot of time in my tiny room upstairs.

*   *   *

"This is where I was becoming angrier," I told Dr. Beal. "I was being bumped all the time. School, home, everywhere. I felt furious and couldn't do anything about it."

"And that makes you feel guilty too?"

"Not in and of itself. I think anyone in my situation would have felt really mad. But I became nasty with it. I said hurtful things. Nana got upset. I'd have big rows with Eleanor about Dean, and

Grandad would jump to Dean's defence. Everyone gave him what-ever he wanted at my expense. And all these memories came flood-ing back as I started going through the old box of stuff, and I became more and more depressed. That's why I'm here. I resented Dean with a passion. To give you just one example of why, I was only allowed two baths a week because of electricity bills, but he got one every night! I was put on a back burner because of him. I lost my Nana to him."

"Are there any positive recollections of life in this new home? Can you think of any at all?" Dr. Beal asked.

I sighed, trying to think of something— anything—good to say about the four years I spent in this cramped matchbox.

"No, but I remember one entertaining event. Occasionally, ev-eryone was in a good mood at the same time. Things would bright-en for a while. One time was just before Christmas, when I got it into my head to please Nana and Eleanor by wearing an old scarlet dressing gown and pretending to be Father Christmas visiting Dean. I just wanted them to approve of me, for once. Nana and Eleanor were delighted and found me some accessories to help. I slowly, noisily, clomped downstairs clad in the red gown, with black belt in the middle and my front stuffed with cushions to simulate plump-ness. With my hair hidden in a Santa hood and my face concealed by a sheet of cotton wool for a beard, I deepened my voice as much as I could and Ho-Ho-Hoed into the living room, where Nana and Eleanor sat with three-year-old Dean.

"'He-eelloow Deeeaaaaann,' I said in a deep Santa voice.

"'Hi, Sheila,' he said.

"Nana and Eleanor couldn't stop giggling for ages."

"So there were occasional good days." Dr. Beal smiled. "You feel awful about resenting Dean, but it sounds like you tried to help out sometimes. That's to be commended."

"I babysat him once a week while Eleanor went for a much-need-ed break, but I did it for her, not for him. I did it because Nana pleaded with me to. She couldn't get upstairs herself, to read him to sleep. Eleanor joined a women's darts team and had a great time during competitions in various pubs. For her sake I took Dean up to bed armed with picture books. I lay beside him in the same way my grandmother had once laid beside me and read stories or chanted poems until he fell asleep. But I never stopped being angry about my needs being pushed aside. He was all-important and I counted for nothing after he arrived. I felt abandoned by Nana. My heart was broken."

15

At home, I took to rolling pastry and peeling potatoes as a way to be useful. I often avoided sitting in the living room, especially if Dean was in it. There was too much tension in there anyway. Nana was moody, only brightening at the arrival of visitors. She'd been out of sorts for some time.

Bobby dropped by often, and so did Antony. Both were living nearby. Their wives Grace and Tabatha sometimes popped in too. Ed, now in the Royal Air Force, came to visit between various postings. For the most part, I didn't talk to any of them unless spoken to, which was not often. They'd come to visit their parents and wanted to talk about their own children, their jobs and gardens. Although I enjoyed listening to them, I felt in the way and usually sat quietly. I didn't want to bore them with my dimwitted conversation.

My mother continued to drive over several times a year with Dad and my half-siblings, or, when she started work, with colleagues with whom she was on nearby business: managers or salesmen. She looked glamorous and gorgeous, always outgoing and bubbly. I was the complete opposite but enjoyed her company and we'd sometimes go to a café. Our conversations usually ended up being about my behavior.

"Sheila, I'm worried about you. Grandad says you seldom speak. Your school reports tell me you're rude to teachers and are absent too often."

"I can't help it if I don't feel well sometimes."

"But you stay off school several days every month. You won't learn anything that way."

"So what? Who cares?" I folded my arms.

"I do. You need to keep going to school, and you have to stop being mouthy with the teachers…"

"You don't know what those teachers are like. Some of them make fun of me or just leave me out. And that's just the teachers. The kids are worse."

"But, She-she, school's only three more years. Try to concentrate. You're clever, and you know you can do it if you try."

"I'm not clever. Everyone knows I'm just an idiot, so why bother? I'm not going to change anyone's mind. All the other kids are good at something, but I'm not. And they all wear nice clothes on the weekends and hang around in big groups, and I hate the way they look at me, like I'm an insect. The girls giggle at me and the boys call me ugly. I'm just fed up with it all."

"Try to ignore them. I know it's hard, but it won't last forever, just until you're sixteen."

"It's lasted my whole life so far. And I hate living at home. I'm always second-best to Dean, so I'm left out there too. Look, I'm not expecting to be first-best, just to be equal. Just to feel they love me as much as they love him. But I know they don't."

"She-she, you'll always be first-best to me. You're my daughter. I wish things had turned out differently when you were younger, and that you'd been living with me all this time. But perhaps when you've finished school you can move in with us. Remember, it's only three more years."

"Every year's like a century here. You don't understand, you just don't."

Mum put her hand on my shoulder and squeezed gently. "I do understand," she said.

I shrugged. Nothing mattered much anymore. And I knew in several hours she'd be driving back out of my life for another few months, and I'd still be stuck with the taunts of school kids and tantrums of Dean.

While I was right about Dean and the horrible kids at school, something did change. I got a crush on Mr. Hoskins, our young, blond

English teacher. This brightened my school day. He told us how cool cigarettes were, and about a film he'd watched in which an actor blew alluring smoke rings across a salon toward an attractive woman. Mr. Hoskins had then learned to blow them. He proceeded to prove it outside in the break, much to our awe. A smoke ring emanated from his lips and rolled forward in silent perfection. I stole a few cigarettes from Grandad's packs in the hopes of one day impressing Mr. Hoskins with smoke rings of my own. I did master them, although I never had the opportunity of showing him.

So, as well as Captain Kirk, Mr. Hoskins now began playing a role in my dreams. I fantasized about being shipwrecked, walking from sea to sand clad in a scant lion-skin outfit, my hair blowing in the wind. I'm wearing knee-high suede boots. Weak from my ordeal, I pass out. Mr. Hoskins finds me and, being stranded himself from an earlier ship, carries me to his wooden hut. I wake to find him admiring me. "Come and eat," he says. "I found coconuts for us." We sit on the beach eating and talking as the sun sets. He hands me a cigarette. I blow a smoke ring.

Unfortunately, my fantasy world didn't help me with my math. More unfortunate was the fact that my math teacher took it personally that I was hopeless in his subject. Mr. Staff would have made a good hanging judge in another life. He had a pointed, stony face and skinny eyebrows that writhed like eels. He always pronounced my name with utter disgust and baited me with questions he knew I was incapable of answering.

I began folding my arms in math class, rolling my eyes and doodling, doing anything other than pay attention to a creep like the aardvark-nosed Mr. Staff. The more he ridiculed me, the angrier I became. I'd tried to explain once that my inability with numbers stemmed from an earlier time in primary school. I'd had scarlet fever for several weeks and missed learning how to divide and subtract. I fell behind and never caught up. Mr. Staff didn't care about this and told me any normal person could do math; it just required common sense. Perhaps I had some marbles missing. The animosity between us grew.

A showdown of sorts occurred one lunchtime when I waited in the middle of the road, intending to cross after a car had passed. I realized Mr. Staff was driving it, and we locked eyes. He turned his steering wheel and drove his car straight toward me. I stood erect, arms folded, head up, holding his gaze. I figured, with perceived teenage immortality, that he wouldn't dare, and I wasn't going to give him the satisfaction of chasing me off the road. He swerved at the last second and I stood my ground in grim satisfaction, smirking after him so he'd see in his rear-view mirror that I knew I'd won.

Shortly afterwards, he announced there would be a swapping of five students from his class and the other, concurrent math class. Some advanced pupils and some needing extra help were going into Mr. Goode's room, and he read out five names, including mine. I'm sure I was the only one needing extra help, but I suppose Mr. Staff was desperate to get me out before he and I killed each other. I found Mr. Goode a supportive and kind elderly man. He chatted to his pupils as if they were adults like him, gaining our complete cooperation and affection. I was happier here and even felt comfortable approaching him for math help.

My stand against Mr. Staff that day made me realize I could stick up for myself when pushed enough. However, I believe part of it was also due to changing hormones and frustration. I was becoming an angry teenager and sometimes lost it with the bullies too, as I did a month later. I'd passed a group of the usual thugs in the corridor when one of them stuck out his leg and tripped me. They all began to laugh, but this stopped as I got to my feet and aimed kicks rapidly at the boy's crotch, forcing him to fend off my boot. I eventually gave up, but I saw fear behind his grin. No one had seen me fight back before. That boy stayed away from me afterwards and never joined in the teasing again. Returning nastiness with like behavior made kids leave me alone.

My outbursts were rare, though. I preferred to walk away from the tough kids and tried to remain unnoticed, but I always wondered why one—albeit provoked—attack toward that boy had earned me his quiet and unexpected regard. Why, I wondered, did it take a few kicks before someone would give me any respect?

The reaction of that one kid didn't change the way the others treated me, and for all my effort to go unnoticed, some things made me stand out as a target. Such as the time Nana insisted on getting me another hearing aid. She explained private aids were better than the clumsy device I'd worn briefly a few years earlier. These new ones could be tucked behind the ear and the sound was better. I was resistant, but I finally went along with it rather than be nagged. And, just as I figured, this hearing aid was more comfortable, but still amplified everything in the classroom. I was forced to listen to the booming noises of chairs banged against desks like rock drummers rehearsing into high-volume microphones; restless feet tapped the floor like woodpeckers hunting for termites; a rude variety of high-pitched sneezes, cackles, coughs, whispers and grunts not dissimilar to a zoo's monkey house. I found it no easier than before to decipher a teacher's voice through this cacophony. In fact it was sometimes quite painful.

Kids noticed the hearing aid and familiar taunts returned. I stopped wearing it. Nana pleaded; Grandad tried to reason with me. Eleanor took me aside and told me Nana paid for the hearing aid out of her own meager savings. It had cost her a lot. I felt guilty, but I couldn't bear wearing it. For a while I put it on in the mornings until I left the house, then threw it into my satchel, but then I was asked where it was when I returned for lunch. So I tried to get accustomed to the thing. But eventually I was becoming so stressed that we all stopped mentioning it, and it found a home at the back of my bedroom drawer.

*   *   *

"I feel guilty to this day, Dr. Beal." I nibbled my fingernail. "Nana tried. Poor all her married life, she'd spent what was for her a huge sum, trying to help. How I wish she were here now so I could cuddle her and tell her I know what she was trying to do."

"You know, I've noticed a pattern," said Dr. Beal. "On your visits here, you may begin with issues surrounding your mother, or neigh-bourhood children or teachers. But it always circles around and back to your grandmother. She was a huge part of your young life. You loved her very much. It's so evident."

"And I craved her love in return." I covered my face with my hands, trying to still my trembling mouth. "To be honest, I felt she had fallen out of love with me—if you know what I mean—after Dean arrived and took my place. But as isolated as I thought myself to be in those days, Nana must have felt I was equally inaccessible to her. But what I needed much more from her than understanding about my hearing difficulties was empathy for the other areas of my life. From everyone, and especially from Nana, I desperately need-ed prominence, direction, tenderness; instead I felt cast out, left to find my own way, ignored."

"You were twelve, thirteen, fourteen years old," Dr. Beal replied. "Most adolescents have turbulent emotions even with a so-called normal life. You were dealing with the impact of way more unstable life experiences than your peers. We'll deal with this, Sheila. It will take time, but I'll help you with it."

*   *   *

Another problem was my shortage of clothes. Kids jeered at me for wearing the same nerdy, raggedy outfit every weekend, and I dread-ed being seen in town. Grandad's money didn't go far and went on food, not clothes. Eleanor was getting something from her ex, but it wasn't much and it all went on Dean. My father, who had been tak-en to court when my mother changed her mind about adoption, had been ordered back then to pay £1 per week toward my upkeep. That may have been worth something when I was a baby, but I was now at high school and he was still sending the same lousy quid. It was enough for half a week's food. I had to wait until my mother was visiting, and she sometimes took me shopping to fit my growing feet for shoes or else bought me a new blouse for school.

One of my greatest treasures, though, was a pair of hot pants my mother gave me for my birthday. They were all the rage in 1970, and nearly every young woman had several pairs. I was happy I had even one pair and got the idea of stealing one of Dean's little jersey tops. He was about four, but his knitted shirt stretched over my small shoulders and chest just fine, ending above my navel. Thus I acquired a skin-tight top to go with my shorts and paraded around town after school feeling like a dancer on BBC's *Top of the Pops*.

"I didn't know it would stay like this," I said sheepishly to Eleanor as I returned Dean's top to her. I'd hoped to sneak it back into his drawer without anyone noticing, but it was permanently stretched and I knew she'd know I had worn it.

Eleanor smiled as if she were recalling something. "You know what," she said. "You can keep it. It goes nicely with those shorts."

I was still close to Tabatha, now married to Antony, and when I became interested in fashion she gave me clothing for birthdays and Christmas. She seemed to know exactly what I liked, and I vividly recall a delicate peach boat-neck with tie-sleeves and a chiffon blouse. If seen by teenagers from school, I was jeered at in my new clothes, but now I began to notice guys in cars blowing their horns and waving at me.

Crude as this behavior was, it did wonders for my self-esteem. It was great walking around in the pair of hot pants on weekends and receiving car beeps and wolf whistles. Instead of feeling insignificant, these were the times I felt worth something. It helped keep me going, in the same way being the Festival Princess had a few years previously.

*   *   *

"Y'know, it's funny, Dr. Beal," I said. "A lot of downs in my life were succeeded by ups."

Dr. Beal raised his eyebrows, as if encouraging me to continue.

"Really," I said, grinning. "People talk about the ups and downs of life, but mine was truly like that, as if I were stuck inside a game of Snakes and Ladders. Wasn't just my moods. I think my luck was

like that. And walking through town getting wolf whistles and beeping horns from appreciative men was definitely an up. They made me
feel pretty, and I was happy for a while."

16

The change in male behavior toward me made me wonder what life in Northingthorpe was like after dark.

Adults dressed up and went to pubs, and I knew from overhearing others at school that even kids my age were allowed out at night. Many met at the youth club to play pool and dance and drink cola. I heard a couple of girls in my class talk about meeting boys for dates. It seemed almost every girl except me had been kissed.

I still had no desire for the boys at school and could not understand the other, prettier girls' fascination with such cretins. However, I was developing a strong urge to cash in on those car beeps and get a date myself. Perhaps I'd bump into a strapping young bricklayer. Or maybe Mr. Hoskins would see me as he drove past and stop to give me a ride. And a kiss.

I asked Nana and Grandad if I could go out some evenings and was given a resounding no. I was too young, only thirteen, never mind if other girls my age were allowed, their parents could decide for them. Nana didn't think kids my age should be permitted out after dark. I asked for Grandad or Eleanor to come for an evening stroll with me, but neither of them wanted to, which was the reaction I expected.

Other kids at school were driven to Middlesbrough's cinema by their parents some nights, or even given tickets to rock concerts. I never got to go anywhere. I was sick of being ignored and of never getting anything.

I pretended to become very interested in music, took Eleanor's record player into my bedroom and set it with several albums to drop, one after the other, for about four hours of Holst's *The Planets,*

Presley's *It Happened at the World's Fair* and some other classical and pop LPs. As soon as the first album was playing, quietly so no one knocked at my door, I climbed out my bedroom window and down onto the stone wall of the back garden. With pounding heart I scuttled around to the side of the house and jumped to the dark freedom of night, terrified all the while that Grandad would suddenly open the back door to let Joss out.

I remember the thrill of that first evening. I'd never walked around Northingthorpe at night, and I spent a few hours skulking around the Hare and Hounds pub to see if Mr. Hoskins came out. It was fascinating seeing some of my neighbours dressed up and walking about town, the men in their best jackets and perfectly coiffed hair, the women in high heels and deep red lipstick. They strode into the pub at eight and tumbled out at eleven with tousled hair and giggles. I sank further into the shadows of the opposite corner as a couple of teachers came out but was disappointed that my gorgeous Mr. Hoskins was a no-show. Slinking home, I climbed back through my window just as the last LP dropped down to play. It was The Beatles' *A Hard Day's Night*.

Further forays took me to the beach, where I perched high on cliffs under the navy blanket of night. The friendly whitecaps of daytime took on a menacing aspect in the moonlight; pale lips curled back and forth over a hungry maw in the gloom.

I began to avoid the beach and took on further voyeuristic activities. I watched girls from my class meet their beloved schoolboys and studied their behavior with the intention of emulating it. Although I knew I'd always be seen as nerdy at school, I was desperate to know what actions were cool so I could eventually behave the same way with, hopefully, Mr. Hoskins.

I saw the girls chortle loudly, flick their hair flirtatiously and lean back onto telegraph poles with one leg bent and a foot supported by the pole, thrusting their hips forward, posing like models in fashion magazines. I saw their boyfriends smirk and strut and lean forward to French-kiss. I made mental notes and crept home to practice posing like a fashionista.

These nightly ventures and my continued fascination for Mr. Hoskins only made me want him to notice me more. My old friend Daniel was in my English class and for some reason was the butt of most of Mr. Hoskins' jokes. The rest of us, under Mr. Hoskins' spell, took to laughing at the teacher's jests, including snipes at Daniel.

He commented on Daniel's habit of stroking his hair back from his face: "Wow, Narcissus is primping."

He smirked at Daniel's way of walking: "See Nureyev here."

He ridiculed the boy's homework.

One day, Daniel was finishing a snack before class, but Mr. Hoskins walked in and the first thing he saw was Daniel thrusting the remainder of food into his mouth. "Won't you see this pig?" he said. Everyone howled, and Daniel looked down.

I grinned at Mr. Hoskins. "He's not a pig," I giggled, "He doesn't have a curly tail."

Mr. Hoskins laughed. "Have you got a curly tail or not?" he boomed.

Daniel continued to look away, and Mr. Hoskins winked at me. I preened and smiled back. However, during the lecture I began to think about what I'd said. I suddenly didn't like myself at all and was not amused at further yarns that afternoon. I stole glances at Daniel, who took notes quietly. At the end of class, he walked out with his friend Paul.

A week later I discovered the repercussions of my remark.

Grandad mentioned at home there'd been trouble in the boys' locker room. The gym teacher was absent and Mr. Hoskins was covering. Apparently Daniel Gloucester had been changing into his soccer outfit when Mr. Hoskins told the other boys he wanted to see if Daniel had a curly tail. He set a group onto Daniel. They bent him over and yanked his underpants so Mr. Hoskins could see whether there was a pig's tail. There was a lot of screaming and hooting. It wasn't even Daniel who told his parents; it was his friend Paul. His mother visited the headmaster to complain, not for the first time, about Mr. Hoskins, and I was horrified that my attempt to impress my teacher had been the cause of this. I'd made a facetious remark about a boy I once used to play with and in doing so I had just done to him what so many kids did to me.

I tried to figure out why I'd said it. Was it resentment that he and I had grown apart? Was it an attempt to make Mr. Hoskins like me? Was it because it felt good to be part of a like-minded group for once? Like-minded? Me? Like them? My mind reeled, but I couldn't discuss it with anyone because I was so ashamed. Besides, with whom could I confide?

Daniel was transferred to another class. Schoolyard gossip was that Mr. Hoskins was summoned to the headmaster's office about the issue. However, any warning he received for his behavior went unheeded and he taught for another year before finally being fired—I heard the last straw was his sexual relationship with a fifteen-year-old girl.

The whole experience taught me how easy it was to slip into the same cruel behavior as the bullies I feared and despised, and I was horrified at the knowledge there was a mean streak in me that was so like theirs.

Discovering this about myself wasn't nearly as bad as what was happening at home. Eleanor's son was allowed to do whatever he wanted with impunity. By now he was sticking a spoon into the jam jar, then licking it and dipping it in again. I complained I didn't want jam that had been fouled by him.

I was told "He's only a child" and "He doesn't understand yet" and "Stop being so selfish." I became angrier with Dean, with Eleanor, with Nana and Grandad. I took to eating dinner in silence, ignoring the brat's squawks for attention. I felt more and more distant from my so-called family.

It didn't help that one day when I took Joss for a walk, she disappeared somewhere in the park. I searched everywhere, behind bushes in case she'd collapsed, on the streets in case she'd been run over, in people's gardens in case she'd been accidently locked in by a gate. After two hours of fruitless searching and calling, I walked home worried sick only to find her lying in front of the warm fire in the living room.

"Oh, she's been back an hour," said Eleanor. "She found her own way home."

Furious, I chased Joss out of the house and into the back garden, where I snatched one of Grandad's bamboo sticks from the vegetable patch and brought it down onto her back. Eleanor called to me in alarm from the back door and I flung the stick and stomped past her and upstairs. Even my dog hadn't wanted to come for a walk with me. It was the ultimate betrayal.

Entering my room, I stopped in horror. My drawers were all open, clothes strewn on the rug, pages from books ripped, colored pens leaking ink onto the floor and scribble on the walls. My favorite paints were opened and mixed together, and my metal swimming cup had a dent in it. I realized instantly that Dean had been playing with my things, and I dashed downstairs, screaming at Eleanor to look at the mess.

She shrugged. "I didn't know he'd been in your room. It's normal for a little boy to be curious. Just tidy it up."

"Tidy it up?" I yelled. "My stuff is ruined. And why should I tidy his mess?"

She continued stirring soup in silence. I dashed into the living room, tears clouding my eyes, and told Nana what he'd done. She shrugged and said he was just a child.

No one cared about me or what was mine. I ran upstairs, screaming continuously. Everything went black in front of my eyes. I grabbed my ruined inkbottles and smashed them against the walls, splattering the custard-yellow backdrop with apple green and shit brown. I stomped on the pens until they oozed blue blood and kicked the furniture, the books and finally the door. It slammed shut and, still screaming, I collapsed onto my bed. I finally slept, and the next morning I went off to school without speaking to anyone.

For several days I tiptoed over the mess to bed and after a while came home to find the broken bottles removed and the clothes folded and returned to their drawers. The remainders of what I had in the world were even more scant than before.

We learned that Ed, his wife Joan and their small daughter would come on a brief interlude from his RAF posting. My grandparents arranged for family and friends to visit for tea during their stay.

Antony and Tabatha arrived first. I'd recently overheard Eleanor telling my mother on the phone that their marriage was in trouble. Tabatha felt Antony's needs were getting in the way of her own. Antony couldn't understand Tabatha's desire to follow a career path. I adored Tabatha and began to worry. She was one of the few people that understood me. I'd sometimes heard her voice a desire to go to art school, and I hoped things would work out.

Bobby and Grace arrived next. Their kids played with Dean, and Eleanor brought in the tea tray. In walked some neighbours and Ed introduced Joan. Tabatha was observing me and I in turn silently watched everyone. Grandad served cake and everyone chatted.

In one of those small lulls, which every conversation has, Tabatha piped up, "Do any of you realize you've all greeted each other and are talking away, but that none of you acknowledged Sheila here?"

I was surprised, because by now I was so accustomed to being invisible that I'd come to expect it. Ed looked guilty, and Joan giggled and said she hadn't noticed me sitting there. Still, neither of them looked at me.

The neighbours glanced at me, startled, and Nana tried to change the conversation, but Tabatha jumped to her feet. "All of you ignore her," she said. "Is it any wonder she is the way she is?" She gazed at me. "I don't know how you stand it," she said, and turning to the others, yelled, "I'm sick of seeing everyone treat her like she doesn't exist." She grabbed her bag and walked out.

Antony shrugged and began asking Grandad's advice on what horses to bet on in the Grand National. Tabatha's comments faded from everyone's mind like a footprint on a windy beach. No one noticed when I sidled to the door and slowly made my way upstairs. I tried to forget the episode, resigned, knowing nothing would change. I read a book in my room and most likely fell asleep for the rest of the afternoon.

Family ties became evident, however, after a shopping errand

Nana sent me on. I was searching the supermarket for gravy powder when I noticed a woman at the end of the aisle looking at me intently. Normally when caught staring, people drop their gaze, but this woman didn't. She continued to watch and I felt myself flush. I poked around some more for gravy and she maintained her study of me until I could stand it no longer. I dodged around another aisle and made for the door. As I did, she walked into my way and stood, arms folded, blocking my exit.

"What's in your hand?" she demanded.

I showed her my list. She reached in my pockets and fumbled around. I noticed everyone staring and I froze, horrified. She obviously thought I'd stolen something. She demanded I open my cardigan. I did so, flustered, and she felt around my waist before letting me leave. Mortified, I sobbed uncontrollably all the way home. When Eleanor heard what happened, she stomped over to the shop, returning to tell us she'd demanded an explanation from the woman, who said I'd been looking at her in a suspicious way. Shoplifters turn around to make sure they're not being watched, the woman explained. To which Eleanor said that anyone who'd been minding their own business and who'd looked up to see a stranger staring continuously would have been just as uncomfortable. She told the manager very sternly that I was only thirteen and, like many teenagers, was very self-conscious and awkward. "My niece didn't need such unspeakable behavior from your staff," Eleanor said.

I received a letter of apology from the store. But more importantly, I was reassured that, arguments aside, we still stood by each other when needed.

Eleanor and I still argued about Dean, but we also, in our calmer moments, went for walks with Joss. During one such outing, I became curious.

"Eleanor," I said. "Why are you divorced?"

"Oh, these things happen," she replied.

Nothing else was forthcoming so I tried again. "Was it something he did? Do you think you'll marry again?"

Eleanor stared at gulls as we walked along the sea wall. There were a dozen of them hunkering behind the old bandstand.

"It would be nice to meet someone one day, but who knows?" She shrugged.

All at once, I felt her aloneness and her determination to make the best of things. With a jolt, it dawned on me that Nana still crocheted clothes and helped me with my English homework, while Eleanor did the family's laundry and cleaning. Grandad worked hard as maintenance manager and still grew vegetables in the garden. What did I do? True, I swept floors and went to the shops and babysat Dean once a week, but I had no regular chores. I was useless at home as well as at school. I made a mental note to be more helpful. It was windy, and as Eleanor pushed Dean in the old stroller he still used for long walks, I threw a ball for Joss. For Eleanor's sake I didn't let on that I now saw her loneliness. I figured she wouldn't want to admit it to a kid like me. The sea hammered the stone walls of the tall promenade and conversation grew difficult anyway.

The roar of the sea became intrusive, violent, and we stopped to watch as waves pummeled the promenade. We walked to the metal fence at the edge of the prom where it jutted out. This portion of the heavy concrete walkway protruded out from the north side near the raw cliffs and from the south side where the beach veered inland a few miles before angling further out to sea. So the first thing the thundering waves hit was the stone wall of the protuberance we were standing on.

Joss nudged my thigh, ball in mouth, and I threw it for her. We watched her bound after it and, to our horror, we watched as the ball got blown over the edge, with Joss squeezing under the railing to follow it. I ran to the bars where she'd disappeared, Eleanor close on my heels and still pushing Dean in his pram. Joss was on the sand twenty feet below, looking up at us as a wave enclosed her and smashed against the concrete. The wave retreated and we located her soaked fur halfway down the sand, being dragged oceanward. She locked eyes in our direction and struggled toward us. The incoming wave helped, pushing her forward to the sand below, then engulfed her again as it smashed against the wall. She began to get dragged out again, powerless against the heavy surge.

"Joss," I shrieked and clambered over the bar.

"No!" said Eleanor, pulling me back. "Quick, the steps over there, get to the sand where the sea doesn't reach. Call her from there. That's the best you can do...hurry!"

I dashed a hundred yards to the stone steps leading to the sand. I had been down these many times as a child to build sandcastles on the mild, silent beach during the many hours when the tide was out and far away and harmless. Now I leapt two steps at a time and ran around the corner to where the sea was again bashing the high walls. There was Joss yet again, clambering up the soggy sand as the sea retreated for the next onslaught. She was still trying to reach Eleanor, high above on the promenade, a distance that was impossible.

"Joss," I yelled. She didn't hear me through the roar of water and I started to inch forward. "Joss!" I screamed with all my might, and now she looked. I bent with my arms out, always my gesture for her to jump up for a hug. She began to run toward me as another large wave crashed down, and then I couldn't see her. The wave pulled back, and I caught sight of her treading water because she was in too deep, being dragged out. She locked her eyes on me. I bent forward again, willing her, and kneeled on the sand, arms outstretched.

I was planning to jump in after her if she didn't get out, but somehow her paws found land and she galloped out of the sea's way toward me, and the next thing I knew my arms and chest were encircling a wet, writhing black body. She stuck her snout in my face, whimpering, and I buried myself in her wet, salty fur. My eyes caught Eleanor's. She was still on the promenade, clutching the pram. She nodded, visibly relieved. My knees felt weak, and Joss's tail was tucked down, her ears pinned back. She trembled all the way home. I did too, but we were all in one piece.

17

Toward the end of my first year of high school I was adopted by a couple of girls in my class, much to my surprise and delight. I finally had new friends. This was good, because my previous schoolmate Caroline was in a different stream and we'd lost touch.

The first of these new friends was Wendy. We were both going on fourteen and took to sitting together during classes after she asked me for spelling help. She caught a bus from out of town and occasionally invited me for sleepovers. A couple of the bullies lived in her village and jeered when they first caught sight of me, but Wendy, tall, streetwise and tough, yelled at them to back off. We hung out at her local youth club. I loved being included, finally, in dances, Ping-Pong, pool and other teenage activities.

At about the same time I made another friend in the form of Lizzie, a freckle-faced girl new to the school. Whenever I wasn't in a class with Wendy, Lizzie parked her tan satchel next to mine, shared my books and pens and sent me funny little notes that made me giggle when the teacher wasn't looking. We began spending time after class drawing cartoons and pictures of pink-lipsticked girls wearing the latest fashions in turquoise and fuschia. Lizzie also lived out of town, in one of half-a-dozen houses that could hardly even be called a village. Her back garden looked out onto fields and the nearest shop was two miles away. I had sleepovers at her place too, and we spent time doodling, watching television and just talking.

Wendy, Lizzie and I spent time together after school. The three of us raced to the park, turned on Wendy's radio and pretended to be Pan's People, dancing on the grass. I then saw them to the bus stop and took the long way home to avoid the gang of gargoyles that always loitered on the sun-bleached old benches at the end of Gate Road. Any time they saw me, they catcalled and chased me, and after a lifetime of it, I was exhausted and would do anything to stay out of their way.

*   *   *

Nana's doctor discovered the kidney trouble he'd diagnosed a year earlier was exacerbated by diabetes and put her on a rigid diet. She had been plump for many years due to her forced inactivity, more so since her almost-permanent confinement to a wheelchair. Within weeks she began to lose weight. This was noticeable even to those of us who saw her every day.

I'd always known Nana as being cuddly and big, but now she was shrinking away; she'd never been so tiny, to the point that the wheelchair seemed overwhelming. The most difficult part for her was avoiding sweets and bread, so much a part of English meals. Dessert was a strong tradition, and suddenly apple pies and other goodies were not allowed. It was hard to imagine how she could stand baking these things for the rest of us when she couldn't eat them herself. Eleanor and I found a shop that sold chocolate for diabetics, and although Nana was not fond of it, at least it was something she could munch on while we tucked into our usual puddings. The doctor expressed satisfaction with her progress and put her on maintenance.

I tried to appear cheerful now even when at my most miserable at home, for Nana's sake. For the most part I succeeded. We laughed at shows on television. I wrote poetry again, sharing it with her and asking for advice. She showed me letters from her pen friends, for she still had many, and we planned my upcoming fourteenth birth-day party.

Lizzie and Wendy came for cake after school for my little cele-bration, and after they left, I helped Eleanor make dinner. Grandad came home and we listened to Nana playing the piano. Mum, Dad, Simon and Wanda came on the weekend with presents. Bob and

Grace came over with a gift, as did Antony and Tabatha. Ed and Joan sent a nice card from Holland, where Ed was posted. So, even though communication was rare these days, the family did still remember birthdays and were kind to me then. Perhaps in their own way, they realized I was going through the awkwardness of teen years and understood. It wasn't that long since they'd been there themselves.

Although Nana and I were starting to get along a little better, we were both just withdrawn in general. I hated the tiny house and always felt a pall upon entering it. Nana was most affected by her aches and pains, but also by the occasional blow-ups still occurring between Eleanor and me, generally over something Dean had done. I confided in my newfound girlfriends more than I did with Eleanor and Nana, and scarcely conversed with Grandad at all. I often stayed in my room when at home.

This feeling was exacerbated during my third year of high school when the students in the first and second years were taking their cue from older kids and debasing me as well. Having now turned fourteen, allowing myself to be insulted by twelve- and thirteen-year-olds was even more humiliating, and one girl in particular, Nadia Hemmings, was especially bratty, sticking out her feet to trip me in the hallways, shoving her bag into my back, remarking on my hair or shoes, or doing anything to make her friends laugh.

One day as I walked past, she said, "Fucking scaredy-cat, you ugly cow."

I had been called worse, but this time something snapped as I saw her tittering with her two friends. I stuck my nose close to hers.

"Who're you calling a scaredy-cat, bitch?" I yelled.

An expression of disbelief crossed her face, but she quickly covered it with a smirk and said, "If you're not a scaredy-cat, then prove it. Fight me."

"Fine," I barked. "Right now!"

Her jaw dropped, and she took a step back. Her friend stepped in. "Not in school," she said. "After school in the park!"

"Fine," I said. "Next week, then. Wednesday in the park."

"Nadia'll be there!" said her friend.

I stormed away. When I cooled off I thought I'd better talk to these girls and just tell them to forget it. But after lunch, to my dismay, the girls in my class began approaching with big smiles on their faces, telling me they'd heard about the fight and would come and watch. The news had whirled around the school faster than a paper kite in a tornado.

Later, some boys in the corridors said they planned to come too. "This I gotta see. You? Fight? Ha!"

The following day, Nadia Hemmings followed me on the way home and tearfully asked to talk to me. "I don't want to fight." She brushed her black hair from her forehead. "I'm really nervous about this."

"I don't want to either, but you blabbed to everyone, so now they all expect it," I said.

"I didn't," she said. "My friends told a few others, then next thing I knew, everyone heard about it. I can't get out of this without looking like an idiot. This is your fault. You shouldn't have made a date to fight."

"No," I said. "It's your fault. You're the one who suggested it. You're the one constantly insulting me. Well, maybe we can just pretend to fight, and not really hurt each other."

"How?"

"I'll pretend to punch you a few times and you pretend to punch me back and then we call it a draw. That way neither of us gets hurt and no one will be able to accuse us of backing out."

"Great idea," she said. "Okay, we'll just gently hit each other, but not really land punches, just pretend like on Batman or something."

Wendy and Lizzie spent the remaining few days trying to talk me out of it, but at the same time they both knew I'd get tormented even worse if I backed out. Wendy offered me advice in how to fight. "Come on, practice with me," she said.

I explained to both of them that the other girl and I had agreed to just pretend for the sake of it, but we weren't planning on really trying to injure each other.

"I'm glad to hear that," said Lizzie.

"Bollocks," said Wendy. "I don't trust her. She's a liar."

"No," I said. "She's scared too, she told me. We've agreed to pretend."

"Come on," said Wendy. "Let me show you how to box." So I went along with Wendy's lessons but knew I wouldn't really need them.

On Wednesday, I was followed by the girls in my class, with my friends at my side. It seemed half the school was waiting in the park. My heart bashed the insides of my ribcage. Nadia Hemmings was already there with her group of friends and made a show of grinning and swaggering, flicking her black bob and swinging her arms in anticipation. The kids circled us. I tried to catch Nadia's eye, but she ignored me and instead snickered with nearby boys, who finally told us to hurry up.

I stood there as Nadia grinned and approached, deciding to let her take the first swing. I suddenly wondered how to fake being punched, but instead of make-believe, she pulled back her fist quickly and landed it full-force on my eye. My glasses smashed and all I could see was red as blood poured out. Unable to see where the blood came from, I fumbled to grab my glasses. I didn't know where they'd landed and knelt to find them as she grabbed my hair and began tugging.

Someone shouted that it was over and Nadia had won. At that, the crowd quickly dispersed, leaving me in the grass, and Lizzie gave me a handkerchief. Wendy, furious, yelled that I should have listened to her and stormed off. My cheeks and hands were a mess of blood, and Lizzie helped clean me up.

"What can I say at home?" I said. "I can't tell them about this."

"Pretend you fell."

With Lizzie's mirror I inspected the damage. My broken glasses had cut my eyelid, but I felt lucky I still had an eye. I was concerned with more immediate problems: how to carry this off at home as if nothing had happened, and how I could face anyone at school again after letting a girl a year younger win a fight. Wendy had been right. I should never have believed Nadia would just pretend to land punches. I'd been fooled and betrayed. Lizzie dashed to catch her bus and I walked home.

The first thing Eleanor said to me when I entered the house was, "What happened?" and the second thing she said after I spouted a story about tripping was, "I don't believe you. Sheila, you were in that fight the kids were gathering for in the park, weren't you?" I tried a few more times to deny it, but both Eleanor and Nana kept questioning me until I admitted the truth.

"How could you?" asked Nana. "Fighting is a terrible thing. What made you do this?"

So I told them the whole story, after which they were silent awhile.

"Sheila," Nana said. "I wish you had told us about this. Grandad would have spoken to someone at the school and stopped this before the fight took place."

"You don't understand," I said. "My life would be worse if he'd done that. I'd have been called a snitch and a coward."

"Well, as it is, you'll be called the loser," said Eleanor. "I want that girl's name. She started this by picking on you and ganging up on you, and by fooling you into just standing there while she took a swing unhindered."

"No," I said. "I can't have you going up to the school. My life there is bad enough. It'll be even worse if it gets around that I snitched on her."

Eleanor kept at me but finally agreed not to go to the school as long as I told her who it was. "I'll go to her parents' home and let them know. Sheila, I insist. If you don't tell me her name, I'll call Wendy's house and question her." So I told her. "I know who she is," Eleanor said. "I know her family and where they live."

I wasn't surprised. Eleanor, with her outgoing nature, knew almost everyone. That evening, Eleanor went over to Nadia Hemmings's home and told her family they needed to have a long conversation with their daughter about bullying, lying, and the fact she could have blinded me. As for me, I had to endure disgusted stares from the other schoolkids and wear broken glasses with only one lens for a month until a new pair arrived. It was the last straw. I'd finally had it.

*   *   *

"Surely by this time your family was well aware of your school troubles," said Dr. Beal. "What conversations did your grandparents have with you about your problems?"

"Conversations? We never had any."

"None of you talked about the kids who were making your life miserable? Or your failing grades?"

"Not really. Oh, I remember one time," I said. "My uncle was standing next to one of my teachers at a soccer match. I guess he told Bobby about my rebellious behavior, because Nana said Bobby told her. She asked me to try and behave at school or else it would reflect badly on the family."

Dr. Beal said nothing. He was too busy making notes and then the hour was up.

18

"Nana, when is Mum coming over again?" This was two days after the fight. "I want to leave Northingthorpe. I just can't live here anymore. I want to go back with her. I'll finish off school in Manchester."

Nana didn't argue. She suggested I call my mother. I did and told her of my unhappiness and that I wanted to live with her. Mum said she'd come the following weekend, so I found a couple of boxes and a suitcase and began packing. I didn't have a lot to pack, but I folded my clothes, leaving out only the school uniform and my jeans to tide me over. I decided to keep what was left of my colored inks and wrapped them carefully, along with favorite books and tapes. I counted the days and asked Nana if she knew anything about schools in my mother's area.

"Don't know, dear," she said. "You can ask her when she comes."

Saturday arrived. I took Joss for a walk, and when I returned I found Mum having tea with Nana and Grandad. Eleanor came in with food, and we sat watching television and eating fish and chips. Afterwards Mum suggested she and I go for a walk. I happily chatted as we strolled along Gate Road. It had been quite a few months since she'd visited, and I looked around the neighbourhood, telling her how glad I was not to have to see it for much longer. Two of the thugs passed on the other side of the street, but because I was walking alongside an adult they refrained from screaming insults.

"Fancy a cake?" asked Mum and I nodded. We found a quiet table at the back of a café and Mum asked me for my account of the fight. I relayed what I'd told Nana and Grandad and mentioned Eleanor had complained to the girl's parents. They had told their daughter to apologize to me, which she had done and left me alone after that.

"What kind of schools are near you?" I asked. "Are you staying overnight, or shall we leave this afternoon?"

"Listen, Sheila," Mum began and put her cup down. She stared at the tablecloth, brushed crumbs away and poured more tea. "Do you recall when you were very little? How I wanted you to live with me and brought you to Manchester? Do you remember it didn't work out, and Nana and Grandad got you back and refused to let you come to live with me again?"

"Yes," I said. "They wanted to keep me away from your other husband, Terry."

"Sheila, that man was the worst mistake in my life, and I've made many," Mum said. "But I can't bring you to Manchester right now."

"I always thought you'd like me to live with you one day." I felt a rock in my stomach.

"Don't ever think I don't want you to. I want it more than any-thing. When I drove over this morning by myself in an empty car ready to pack your things and have you next to me driving home, the last thing I thought was to be having this conversation with you. She-she, you were out when I arrived. I was so excited. Imagine my shock when your Nana began telling me to let you down gently, to explain to you your place is here in Northingthorpe, that they'll look after you no matter what and that this brawl episode will blow over and be forgotten as soon as the next couple of kids fight."

I just stared at her. "I can't stay here," I said. "I've packed my bag and some boxes. I'm ready to go."

"Sheila, listen to me." Mum wore that extremely sad expression I sometimes saw. "When my Mum and Dad got you back the last time, they were very angry with me. You had been so mistreated, and I'd been too busy working fulltime and raising baby Jeanette to really notice what was happening to you. And that bastard was so good at covering his tracks. I had no idea what he was doing to you all day. But my parents accused me of neglect, reminded me they'd begged me not to take you in the first place and said my decision had left you deeply disturbed. It's true I should have seen how unhappy and terrified you were, but I had waited a long time to have you live with me, and I suppose I just closed my eyes to your needs. I hoped you'd get used to the new home. Another mistake!"

She rested her elbows on the table and cupped her head in her hands. We both just sat awhile.

"The other thing I hadn't realized back then was how much you filled an empty space in my Mum's life," she continued. "My brothers and sister and I were her world. She doted on us but we were growing up, beginning to live our own lives, move away, marry. Mum's legs were getting worse and she was pretty much confined to the house. Then suddenly she had you to care for: a new little girl who needed her. In her moment of despair as her legs became weaker, you came along and gave her another reason for living. And you both bonded so strongly that when I returned for you, I was too late. I took you anyway, but I was too late and I hurt you both."

Numbly, I told my mother I really wanted to leave Northingthorpe and that Nana didn't require my presence any more. "She hasn't needed me for the last few years," I said. "Since 'dear little Dean' arrived on the scene, he's been the sole object of her doting, let me tell you. She won't miss me much, if at all. In fact she'll be glad I'm gone."

"Not true! She loves you as much as she ever has. Don't shake your head—she does, Sheila. Yes, she also has little Dean around, but one child doesn't replace another."

"You're wrong," I said. "You're really wrong. He comes first all the time. He gets everything he wants. I can't even take more than two baths a week, because of the electricity bills, and he has one every night. Anytime I'm ever talking to her about anything, she stops listening as soon as Dean screams for her attention. I'm second-best all the time and I hate school and the mean kids there and I want to leave. Nothing goes right here. I want to leave!"

"Sheila, I can't take you. I really want to, but I dare not do this. I'm so afraid she'd never speak to me again. I promised after last time that I'd never repeat it, and she reminded me of that today.

It would destroy your Nana. Yes, it would, Sheila. I can't do this to her at her age. She's ill, you know this. Please be patient. You and I have all our lives ahead of us, and I promise one day you will come to live with me. But your Nana is getting on and may not have many more years."

I stared at the mustard-and-mud-patterned carpet. *Such a crappy color for a carpet*, I thought. *I guess I'm stuck with this stupid café. And this stupid town.*

"Dear girl, I want you to know I really had intended to take you with me. I was already looking into nearby schools. I didn't know until I arrived today that your Nana simply assumed I'd reason with you, that she felt so strongly you should stay. But please know the fact you asked me to come—that you actually want to live in my home with me—has made me very happy. I never knew if I'd ever hear you say it. One day the time will be right."

When we arrived home, Nana was at the dining room table, cutting carrots on a chopping board. Grandad came in from the back garden with a bowl of freshly picked gooseberries and Mum offered to make them into a pie. Eleanor and Dean were in the living room watching a children's show. Everything seemed so normal, but I felt like the sky had fallen in. I had already become used to the idea that I'd be gone after this weekend. Realizing I'd still be here, and that I had to continue to sit in a class day after day with the same horrible kids as well as play second fiddle at home was almost too much. I was very quiet through dinner.

Mum left the following day, and I remained subdued. As she drove off, Nana waved from the front window, and Eleanor and I stood at the gate, watching the car disappear. Eleanor nodded at me, anxiously. "Okay?" she asked. I nodded automatically.

Something changed in me after that. I seldom talked to anyone unless spoken to first. I continued to watch my couple of pop shows on television, do chores I was asked to do and eat with the family as usual. I sat in class and took notes and wrote essays. However, I was often asked if I was listening or not, and usually found myself just staring out the window or at a wall, thinking of absolutely nothing.

I tuned out the bitchy girls, the snide boys, the irritated teachers, and if I heard them at all, I no longer cared what they said. I was moody too. I began to squabble with Lizzie, then with Wendy, and we'd make up and break up as friends, sometimes two of us ganging up against one, then swapping sides. I didn't hang around as much with Wendy. I lay on my bed and did nothing. I was unable to enjoy anything, even reading.

I hated Dean. He was the primary cause of my misery at home. I had lost Nana to him several years ago, and even more than ever felt I had to avoid him or go crazy, but because he ran all over the house, my bedroom was my only retreat. I took to staying upstairs, mad with the misery of rejection.

Summer leaves fell and flocks of birds passed overhead. They, at least, could migrate. Snow arrived.

I heard talk of Nana needing more medical care and she was admitted to the hospital for several weeks. Various relatives came to Northingthorpe more frequently and Mum visited often. I babysat Dean in the evenings while Grandad and Eleanor spent time at the hospital. Other times I'd go with Eleanor, or with Mum and Grandad, who explained to me the seriousness of the situation: as well as diabetes and failing kidneys, Nana now had cancer. Mum and Grandad sat me down and explained that Nana was not expected to survive. They were arranging for her to be moved back so she could die at home, surrounded by family.

In the meantime, we continued to visit her, but everyone felt Nana shouldn't be told of the seriousness of her illness. It would be a horrible thing for her to be told she was not going to make it, and the family asked me to be careful not to say anything to make her guess. I understood, it being common in those days. People often felt it was better to pretend everything was alright, so as not to upset or scare the ill person. A few years later I watched *Love Story*, in which the same thing happened. In one scene a doctor told the husband, Oliver, that his wife Jenny was terminally ill, but she herself wasn't told. So it was, in this case, I found myself frequently weeping in the school's toilet cubicles or in my room at home, but extremely careful to act cheerful when at Nana's bedside.

On one visit, I arrived with my mother to find Nana distressed because of one of the nurses. Unable to walk or even get out of bed, Nana had asked the nurse on duty for a bedpan and had been told to wait until tea was served to the other patients in the dormitory, so Nana quietly sipped from her mug and waited. However, the bedpan did not arrive, and after half an hour she rang her bell. The nurse approached and when asked again became irritated, snapping at Nana to be more patient.

"I can't drink all this tea and not need to go, you know. And now I'm a nuisance to her," Nana sobbed.

I stayed with her while Mum went to find the nurse. I dreaded my mother making one of her scenes, but she didn't. She later told me she was determined to stay calm; otherwise Nana would suffer after we'd left. The nurse arrived. Mum smiled and said something nice to her. The curtains were pulled, and we didn't leave until Nana was in better spirits. I could understand why everyone wanted her to come home. Who needed to be in a place like this with a mean-spirited nurse?

The next day, I thought up the idea that Nana might like to hear her favorite song, "Windmills of My Mind." I decided to record it and take it to the hospital.

I knew Antony had an LP with the song on it, so the next time he was in the house and sitting dejectedly at the table with Eleanor and Grandad, I approached him, something I'd avoided doing for a long time, but this was important. I asked to borrow the LP. He scowled at me, which I'd expected. I explained I wanted to add the song to my audiotape. He scrunched his face as if in the presence of a mangy dingo. And for once my wall crumbled, I let his loathing wash over me and my voice faltered. I retreated to the kitchen, where I stared out the window. I heard Grandad explaining my intention was to take the recording to the hospital to cheer Nana. Antony did at least feel guilty enough to come out and tell me he'd bring the record very soon. He even patted my shoulder, and I tried not to cringe from his touch.

A few days later I carried my tape player to the hospital, accompanied by some of the family. "Surprise, surprise," I said in a cheerful voice. Nana listened to the song and smiled politely, but I could tell she was not happy. Years later it dawned on me that my overly benevolent behavior had likely caused her to become suspicious. I recall that visit and the silent, circumspect look she gave us all as we bobbed our heads and smiled and chattered endlessly. At the end of visiting time, she asked my mother to remain a few moments, so Grandad, Eleanor, Dean and I waited in the lobby until Mum met us, ashen-faced. She wouldn't tell us what happened until we arrived home.

"What did she say?" we asked as soon as we got in. "What's wrong?"

"She said, 'Viv, if anyone will tell me the blunt truth, it's you. Tell me now. Am I going to die?'" Mum gripped her hands together as we all froze, horrified.

"What did you tell her?" asked Grandad.

"I...this is the first time I've lied to her. I just was not expecting the question and didn't know what to do. And I couldn't tell her the truth. I simply couldn't say it. I shook my head and said no. But I don't think she believed me, and now I feel terrible. I think she knows I lied to her."

"Why do you think that?" asked Eleanor.

"Because she then said to me, gently but firmly, I was to promise her that if she died, I was to burn all her diaries."

"What?" I cried. "You can't burn her journals. They'll be precious memories of her." In my mind I saw Nana clearly. Every day, all her life, she had written reams in her large diaries. Details of what was happening for this or that person, what she thought and felt, her ideas for letters-to-the-editor and poems, her hopes and memories. Funny things, sad things, day-to-day stuff. I'd never tried to read them, but she had occasionally read excerpts to me.

"Sheila, I've made a solemn promise to her. I can't break it."

"But..."

"Don't you see? Those are her personal diaries. There are likely things written that are very private. Maybe her fears or disappointments, perhaps some personal secret about some member of the family, possibly a few things that might hurt some of us. If she's not comfortable with our keeping them, she has her own reasons and we must carry out her wishes. The fact that it was the first thing she asked of me tells me this is important to her. She wants those diaries gone when she's gone."

Mum stopped and sighed. I suddenly remembered Nana once telling me one's word is very important. A promise is a promise: a solemn thing to give. I knew Mum would keep her word to Nana. We'd all been brought up that way.

"I had to tell her to not be silly, that we hoped she'd be around for a long time yet, and I'd only take the diaries with me to put her mind at rest. That I looked forward to returning them to her once she'd fully recovered. But I'm to collect them all and take them home. And I'm not to read them. That goes without saying."

We all sat immersed in our own thoughts. My mind was full of Nana, lying in that hospital bed, wondering if she was dying.

Mum wept, closing her eyes. "'Am I going to die?' she asked me! I'll never forget it."

Not long after, Nana was brought home, and for the most part she lay propped in bed in the living room. She caught up on letters, crocheted cushion covers and insisted Eleanor bring the loaf each day so she could slice it and butter the bread for dinner. As usual, she always gave Grandad the crust, his favorite part.

We all sat together in the evenings watching comedy shows. I made an extra effort to get along with Dean, keeping him amused upstairs whenever Nana looked too tired or when Eleanor and Grandad were busy helping her in and out of bed. On her good days, she sat in her wheelchair, happily encouraged by being mobile. I sometimes came home from school to see her little face peering through the window, watching for me through the glass as she used to.

Sometimes I stared with yearning at her shrunken frame as Nana began to spend more and more time sleeping. I wanted so much to pick her up and wrap her in my arms like she did for me when I was small; to rock her gently and sing to her. She was now taking prescribed pills for pain, and the front window more often was dark and empty as I walked up the garden path. I missed her terribly. It began to dawn on me that I had missed her for the last five years. That is how long it had been since the chasm had opened between us, and perhaps it was this that made me ask one night if I could sleep in the bed with her like I used to when I was small.

Grandad overheard and was against it. "It's just a single bed, Sheila, not the big roomy one at Felicity Close. And you're not tiny anymore."

I begged Nana to let me sleep over with her, just once. She said yes, and that evening I climbed in, careless enough to bump her as I lay down. She moaned in pain, and Grandad rushed over in alarm.

"Sheila, this won't work," he said.

"I didn't mean to hurt her," I said. "Nana, are you okay? I'll be very careful. Can I stay?"

Nana nodded, her eyes closed. Grandad hesitated, said goodnight and turned out the light. For the first time in this house, I experienced sleeping downstairs, and it was strange and lonely, not the same experience as in the other house. Nana must have felt like this until she got used to it. As well, the streetlights shone in a little through the gap in the front window's curtains, and the occasional late-night car flung its headlights in to swirl around the walls like startled wraiths as the vehicle turned the bend. I experienced nothing like this in my own room upstairs, because it was facing the back.

The night was not a successful one. Nana was silent and asleep, assisted by the pills, while I was wide-awake for hours. I lay there remembering the hundreds of stories Nana had read to me years ago: me lying with my little head on her shoulder, turning the pages, giggling and asking questions nineteen to the dozen. I thought of the times we had lain in the big bed thinking up joint poems, or playing noughts and crosses, squiggles, snakes and ladders. I recalled our watching late-night television together when everyone else was asleep, me holding on to her for dear life at the scary parts of *The Outer Limits*. She'd nod and reassure me, wrap me in her cuddly arms and smile. She rocked me and sang to me. And now here I was, staring at my Nana as she lay unresponsive, unconscious, unreachable.

I realized that night more than I ever have since how relentless time is, how all things pass and are never the same. How you cannot ever reach back through time and space and retrieve what you had. When something is gone, it is gone.

19

Mum stayed over often, leaving Dad in Manchester with Simon and Wanda. Bobby and Antony visited every day, and other relatives came when they could.

I stayed in the background, silent and upset at the sombre mood and hushed voices. One time, about to return to school after lunch, Nana said something about a long-past event to Grandad. I saw him smile and nod at her, then leave the room quickly, and when I opened the front door to leave, I saw him sitting at the end of the dining room table, facing the corner, sobbing uncontrollably. It was the first time I'd seen his stoic façade break, and I walked over and rested my hand on his shoulder. "Grandad?" I said. "Can I bring you anything?"

He shook his head vigorously, still sniffling into his hands, and managed to croak, "Just get to school, you'll be late." I left, feeling impotent, telling Eleanor, who was in the garden, to go in.

Nana slept most of the time now, and whenever she was awake we were unable to talk to her. She seemed to think Mum and Eleanor were children again, and spoke to them as such. The same was true for everyone except Grandad, with whom she still talked normally. I was someone she didn't often recognize.

Nurses came in and out, and then one day I came home from school and Mum told me the doctor had announced that Nana would not last the night. She lay in her little bed in the living room with her eyes closed as we ate in the room next door, not tasting our food, not even really hungry. Even Dean appeared subdued, although he was too young to understand. Later I sat on the floor in the living room reading a book to him. Bobby entered, face tight, and walked to the end of the room. He stood silently gazing at his mother for a long time, and although I glanced at him once, I then kept my eyes firmly planted on the book and continued to amuse Dean, giving Bobby the privacy he needed for his silent reverie. He finally walked back out of the house without talking to anyone. I think he couldn't.

I can't recall how we spent that last evening, except a lot of the family came in and out. I know I asked to stay up, but Mum, Eleanor, and Grandad insisted I get some sleep. They would sit at Nana's side but said I was too young and I needed to go to bed. I guessed it meant they really didn't want me around to worry about, so I stood for a while gazing at Nana before I went upstairs. I tucked myself into one of the two beds in Grandad's room, which I was sharing with my mother—Grandad was using my space—and I lay awake a long time, trying to hear conversation from downstairs, but at last fell asleep.

It was full daylight when I awoke. The first thing my eyes took in was my mother standing nearby, staring quietly out of the window, tears travelling slowly down her face. Her bed hadn't been slept in. I figured she must have been crying a long time for her tears to be so slow now. Her arms were folded, and the sun highlighted her uncombed blonde hair. I thought how pretty she was, even with no sleep. I did not speak. I didn't want to hear it yet. I continued to look at her awhile, then closed my eyes. I finally opened them again to find her facing me, but I said nothing as she sat on the bed to tell me. I just nodded, and we remained there a short while. She asked if I wanted some tea. I nodded again and she left. I washed, dressed, then sat on the bed, not wanting to go downstairs or see anyone, but she came up with the tea, so I drank it. She asked if I was alright and I told her I was and I'd come down soon. She left me with instructions not to enter the living room. "We're all sitting in the dining room," she said. "Come and join us there."

I remained motionless on the bed, not thinking of anything—it was like my brain had been extracted. My heart felt like a fossil. I sat there a long time until Mum came in with Eleanor and they said something, but I simply nodded. Grandad popped up behind them, and he said something too. I nodded again. Feeling crowded, I followed them downstairs, hesitating at the bottom.

I glanced at the closed living room door, and Mum put her arm around my shoulder, herding me into the dining room. They were bustling about now, washing dishes, amusing Dean, letting Joss out, normal things needing to be carried on. Bobby appeared. Then someone else dropped by, and then some other person. I didn't really notice. I wandered into the kitchen, talked about inconsequential things and eventually found myself heading back upstairs to sit on the bed. After a while Eleanor came and asked if I was okay. She hovered a while then left me alone.

I lay on the bed, slowly allowing thoughts to return, but they were of flying through space with Captain Kirk, then of the Osmonds' latest song, and then of a recent conversation I'd had with Lizzie—anything but what was happening in this house right now and anything except imagining Nana lying stock still directly beneath me. Mum came up again, and I listened as she talked to me—she was saying I needed to cry, to let it out. I just stared at her. She was like a cardboard cutout to me, but I felt bad about not showing more emotion. I tried to smile, and she left again. I moved to the window and looked out at the grass, the road, the trees and sky. Clouds shifted and a callous sun spliced the glass pane. I squinted and allowed my thoughts to empty out again.

Next thing, Antony knocked on the door. I glanced at him as he walked in, then turned back to the window. He stood next to me and I ignored him, not out of spite but because I was unable to respond. He talked softly about the fact that we all deal with these things in our own way, but how the folks downstairs were very worried about me because I wasn't behaving normally. "It's okay to cry," he said. "We all are. We're all heartbroken. Your Nana loved us and we loved her and we're all going to miss her." And, listening to his words, his endless chatter about Nana, I finally let her into my mind in a rush and broke down, big time. He led me downstairs, hugging me, and delivered me to my mother.

Inside, I was angry at myself—of all people, why let Antony be the one who managed to unhinge me? The others, however, looked relieved, and when Antony said he needed to do some errands, he asked me to come along. I refused, but Mum begged me to go with him. When I still wouldn't, Grandad and Eleanor asked if I'd help them out by buying some groceries. They were too tired to go. So I went off with Antony, pausing halfway along the street to peer back at the house. The living room windows were fully open, and the curtains were blowing out through the frame. By the time we returned, the window was closed and Nana was gone.

The next couple of days are hazy now. I remember only two other things from this time. The first is, after a full day of listening to various relatives coming in and talking about their visit to the funeral parlor, I decided this was something I wanted to do. In the evening when Mum, Eleanor, Grandad and I sat in the house, I announced my need to visit Nana.

Eleanor was horrified. "You can't," she said. "It'll shock you."

I stomped my foot and insisted I be taken or go by myself.

"Sheila," said Eleanor, "Nana doesn't look like she did in life. You don't know what you're doing."

"I know what to expect," I said. "I read, I watch the television, I know about the pallor, the stiffness, I have read all about that. I have to visit her." My voice dropped to a hoarse whisper. "I need to talk to her."

Mum broke in. "Eleanor, if we don't let her, she won't get another chance and might never forgive us. Come on, let's take her over."

During the five minutes it took the three of us to walk through the lamp-lit streets, I wondered what I'd say. I knew I wouldn't be getting a reply and felt unsure how I'd handle that. The parlor was down a back alley, part of the same building as the Hare and Hounds I'd once stared at with curiosity during my phase of exploring the town at night. The pub held no fascination for me now; it was a booze-smelling, smoke-filled room and I couldn't care less what went on inside.

Eleanor had a key for the parlor. She unlocked it, and I stood outside the door, staring at two unlidded coffins. The nearest one had a plastic cover over the body and two hoses coming out of it, hissing air into a wall fan. I mused briefly that the body must not be fresh but put the thought out of my head immediately. Mum and Eleanor entered the room and walked slowly to the coffin at the other end. They turned to me and I joined them, staring at the wall. I couldn't bring myself to look yet. In my peripheral vision I saw Eleanor's hand reach for the sheet.

"Are you ready?" she asked.

I nodded and continued staring at the wall while she pulled the cloth away. I brought my eyes down one painful inch at a time until they rested on Nana's pale countenance. I felt like my throat and chest were going to split open. Eleanor said something but I couldn't hear. My dear grandmother was my sole focus.

"Nana," I whispered, "I love you." I reached my hand to her. Mum and Eleanor moved toward me, talking, and I yelled at them. "Get out," I screamed. "Out! Leave me alone."

"Sheila," Mum cried. "Please..."

"Leave me alone. I want to talk to my Nana. Out!" I turned, clawing at the air, pushing them away. "Go!"

"Okay, okay, call us if you need us. We'll walk back and forth in the alley," Mum said, and she and Eleanor left.

I stormed to the door and slammed it shut, still screaming, then stopped, panting, and walked back to Nana. There she lay, her beautiful round face completely still, her eyelids slightly open, revealing part of her lovely blue eyes underneath. With horror I realized her irises had sunk a little, so that they seemed to be pointing in slightly different directions. I raised my fingers to my lips, kissed them and stroked her forehead. I kissed my fingers again and ran them along her cheek. And then I talked. And I talked, and I paced the room, returning to look at her and pace the room again, talking endlessly, and to this day I cannot remember a single thing I said. I just know it was important.

After a while the door opened, and Mum and Eleanor began to come in, but I swung around howling at them to go, that I wasn't finished yet. They retreated hastily just as I flung myself at the door to slam it shut, and I continued to pace, to clutch my hair, to talk and talk until I dwindled into a heap on the floor, exhausted, still muttering. This time, when Mum and Eleanor entered, I did not resist as they helped me up. I quietly waved goodbye to my Nana, and we went home.

The second thing I recall is the day of the funeral. Everyone gathered at the house, and the hearse parked in front, followed by several black cabs. Relatives began piling into the taxis while Eleanor clambered into the back of the first cab and helped her grief-stricken father in. Mum climbed in close on his heels but there was not enough room for me.

"You'll have to sit in front," Mum said, so I sat alongside the silent driver as the procession began.

A glass partition prevented any communication between them and me. At one point I turned around to see Grandad sobbing, hugged from both sides by Mum and Eleanor, also in tears. I turned back around, totally alone, but refusing to show my feelings in front of the stranger sitting next to me. I fixed my eyes on Nana's coffin just a few feet ahead as we drove around Northingthorpe.

At the church, I got out as the driver ignored me and opened the back door for the other three. Mum stepped onto the pavement and held out a hand for Grandad who was closely followed by Eleanor. They wrapped their arms around each other and began moving toward the coffin that was now being lifted by my uncles.

Various relatives and friends huddled with their young families. Dean stood with Bobby's children. Grace watched over them, getting them to join hands while Bobby walked to the hearse. I stood awkwardly, not knowing what to do.

There were many passersby on the street quietly standing to attention out of respect, but I felt conspicuously alone as I stood and watched Nana carried up the churchyard's path by my uncles, followed by Grandad, Mum and Eleanor. Everyone began making their way toward the church, immersed in their grief and hugging each other, but I felt myself being left behind, immobile. I simply could not walk up there all by myself. All of a sudden, Tabatha appeared in front of me and held out her arms. I collapsed into them, hid my face in her chest and was finally able to walk.

*   *   *

"So you see, Dr. Beal, I really was invisible. I still feel invisible." Dr. Beal scribbled continuously.

"I just never fit in, anywhere. And I still need Nana. I want her back. I really, really want her here, right now. I need to talk to her about everything. And I can't. It's too late."

He handed me a box of tissues and put down his notepad. "Sheila, although she cannot be here, you can still talk to her. Pretend she's sitting right there in the corner chair. What would you say to her?"

"Well, she's not sitting in it, so what's the point?"

"It'll help you explore your thoughts about this event and the sense of estrangement. Just try it. Let's see what comes. Imagine she's come back to visit you, here and now, and is waiting to hear you."

I looked at the empty chair.

"No. I simply can't. First, I'd feel silly talking to someone who isn't there, and second, I can't pretend even for a minute that she is there."

"Okay. But I'd like to give you some homework to do before we next meet. I know your hobby is writing. I'd like you to write a letter to your grandmother. Pretend you can send it to her, wherever you imagine she is now. Can you do this and bring it with you?"

"Maybe. I'll try."

I did write a letter to her. The first since I was a child. As I began, I imagined it would be a loving note telling her how much I missed her, how I enjoyed our poetry projects when I was a kid, that sort of thing. And the first paragraph was like that. But as I continued writing, faster and more furiously, I was shocked at the poison pouring out of me. Truly shocked. Dr. Beal was not. And he and I began to work intensely on the emotions I had finally acknowledged.

*   *   *

After the funeral, I continued at Northingthorpe school for a short while until Mum arranged a new one in Manchester.

Grandad, Eleanor and Dean stood in the garden, and I said goodbye. "Mum and I will come to visit next year," I said. My mother walked to the car with yet another box and I dashed back inside to grab my jacket. I was surprised to see tears rolling down Eleanor's face as I came back out. I thought she'd be glad to see the nuisance—me—leave. She and Dean stood hand-in-hand in the garden and I walked over to Dean awkwardly, patted his shoulder and nodded at Eleanor. I felt rather hollow. Grandad tried to smile and I mumbled something. We all waved to each other until the car turned the bend, and we were gone.

20

Annual summer vacations with my mother and her family hadn't prepared me for moving to Manchester and living with them.

My emotions ran the gamut from chronic grief over Nana's death, to bewilderment over my second step-dad's bizarre behavior, to frustration over the pandemonium of my much younger half-brother and sister and their noisy friends, to confusion over finding my way around a large metropolis, to fear in a new school full of sophisticated city kids. I was lost.

It all happened so quickly. That I'd never again return to Nana was poetic irony. I had been desperate to leave Northingthorpe—not without good reason—but Nana's death caused me to sink like a boulder. I was unsure how to break to the surface.

The house was the one I'd been coming to for holidays over the last few years: a brick terrace on a small, suburban street with little traffic. This could have made for peace and quiet except that the back garden looked down a steep, narrow valley onto railway tracks way below. The trains, mainly freight, were only occasional as opposed to the more frequent passenger carriages on other lines, but they tended to lumber by in the middle of the night or during dinner. The sheer tonnage of their cargos caused the homes and pavements to vibrate and groan. Surprisingly, I found this comforting. The trains reminded me of earlier times and I sometimes leaned over the fence to watch them go by.

Although I became accustomed to our house vibrating every time a train rumbled by, I learned after eventually having friends for sleep-overs that I needed to warn visitors about these disturbances, for one of them told me the next morning she thought an earthquake had occurred in the middle of the night.

Mum chose a girls' school halfway across the city, because at that time the nearby secondary school had a bad reputation. She took me to meet the headmistress, who left me with a teacher in a classroom. I sat in an empty desk at the front, surrounded by curious eyes. When the teacher left to get papers, two girls behind me tapped my shoulder and smiled.

"I'm Babs," said a pleasantly plump blond girl. "And this is Mandy."

"Hello, I'm Sheila," I croaked. I'd been up most of the night with attacks of nerves. However, these kids seemed nice enough and introduced me to girls behind them.

"Where've you come from?" Mandy asked. She wore huge spectacles in a small pale face. "You have an accent."

Those at the other side of the classroom began asking questions such as why did I move, what was my house like, which part of the city did I live in. I had bad vibes about this other group. They stared with slitted eyes and slight smirks on their faces, chewing gum and preening themselves in little mirrors, which disappeared quickly when the teacher re-entered the room. During the break, these girls surrounded me outside, demanding answers to this and that question, but their attitude set me ill at ease and I knew it showed. I stood as stiff as a meerkat surrounded by jackals.

The girls quickly tired of me, turned their backs and wandered off to stare at the boys' school at the other end of the soccer field. I stood alone as I had so many times in Northingthorpe, expecting at any moment to be laughed at or insulted, but thankfully the bell rang and we all went inside.

The next few months proved my impressions accurate. I was befriended by Mandy, Babs and their nerdy but nice little group and bullied by Sally, Janet and their clique. I concentrated on the positive: my new friends. I began visiting Mandy's house on weekends. She was an ardent hiker and her father dropped us off on walking trails and collected us a few hours later. Sometimes other friends joined us, except for Babs who utterly refused to tramp about the countryside. Instead, she saw us afterwards for supper, or we'd meet at her house on rainy Saturdays and dance to Tamla Motown.

Mandy and I also went window-shopping in the town center where her mother worked in a food market. I liked her mother; she reminded me of a younger version of my grandmother. She wore an iron caliper on her leg just as Nana had many years earlier, and she had an industrious nature, again similar to Nana, always rushing to help customers at the market or cooking and cleaning at home for her family. Watching her limp around made me realize how energetic my grandmother must have been, to care for all her children and keep house in a time when poverty kept modern conveniences out of reach. It dawned on me how much Nana had achieved, and the realization made me miss her even more.

Occasionally Mandy came to my house, as did Babs. None of us lived close, for although we went to the same school, we lived in various suburbs of the sprawling city, so we were constantly cadging rides from our parents on weekends or catching buses to meet in the centre.

I couldn't figure out, however, why yet again it was my lot to be picked on at school. Sally's gang didn't speak to Babs or Mandy, but neither did they harass them. There was something about me mean kids homed in on and I found that, just like in Northingthorpe, I became a target.

I wasn't the only one, though. The young art teacher also was tormented, sometimes beyond endurance. Fairly new on staff, she found any attempt to teach color theory, sketching or clay modeling was met with contempt by these girls. In art class they sniggered, mimicked, and folded their arms. My friends ignored them and paid attention while the teacher valiantly lectured in spite of the scorn. But while my group obediently painted still life, the others turned their backs and rolled their eyes. They never dared display such disdain in classes run by older women. It got so Miss O'Riley began wearing an expression of dread on Wednesday afternoons when our class walked into her studio. Sally's gang detected her weakness and as the weeks went by they became more disruptive.

It occurred to me that I was like Miss O'Riley, soft-hearted and weak. I wondered how I could change myself. After a lifetime of turning the other cheek it wouldn't be easy.

I first became aware of Colleen in a joint class held each week. We all gathered around long tables and she sat diagonally across from me, next to girls in her group. She had a lazy eye but a pretty face, shiny brown hair and great teeth. The teacher was late one time, and all of us were chatting across the table, but Colleen seemed to be on her own. I began to listen as she attempted to catch the attention of girls on her right and then on her left, to no avail. She kept saying "Did you hear the one about..." and a couple of girls listened for a few seconds as she launched into a joke, but then they thought of something else to tell each other and turned to talk to their friends, and Colleen attempted to relay her story to other classmates with the same result.

At last she threw back her head and laughed to herself, muttering in a husky voice, "Oh man, no one wants to hear my joke!"

I liked her at once and said I wanted to hear it. Delighted to gain an audience, she told me the funny story, which I have long since forgotten, but we grinned at each other and later she caught up with me after the final bell.

"Hey, man, I'll walk you to the bus," she said. "I don't catch one myself, cuz I can walk home in half an hour." She had an unusual way of walking: sort of half-strutting and half tip-toeing in a way I'd never seen anyone else do.

After a month of waving at each other in corridors between classes and walking to the bus stop after school, Colleen asked if I'd like to meet her boyfriend.

"Pete has the day off, so he's picking me up at lunchtime. We're going for fish and chips."

"Okay—I'll walk you over."

Two motorbikes revved at the school gates, each with a leather-booted, Belstaff-wearing teenager astride it. Colleen introduced me to the nearest one.

"Hi," said Pete. A friendly grin, skin-tight jeans and long hair revealed to me someone who couldn't be more different from the skinheads in Northingthorpe. "This is my neighbour, Craig."

I turned to nod at the guy on the other motorbike. Craig reminded me of Davy Jones of The Monkees. He had a cheeky grin, dark hair that buried his ears and neck in the 1970s style, and his brown eyes gazed openly into mine with a jovial expression. He looked cool. They both did. *Wow*, I thought. *They're like rock stars. And they're actually smiling at little me.*

"Hello." I said. "Um, well, have fun. See you later, Colleen."

"Hey, why don't you come? Maybe you can ride on the back of Craig's bike," said Colleen.

I shook my head. Suddenly shy, I didn't wish to put Pete's friend on the spot. Perhaps he didn't care to give me a ride. "I need to finish my assignment before class," I lied. I waved and left.

* * *

My mother was delighted I'd made friends. She'd initially introduced me to a couple of girls nearby, but we hadn't clicked and lost touch quickly. I think she worried that I might become as unhappy at this school as I had been in Northingthorpe's, so she relaxed when I began talking about Mandy and the others. She bought me second-hand hiking boots and drove us to a couple of new trails and picked us up later. She found a skirt pattern and took me shopping for fabric, promising to sew me a couple of mini-skirts for the weekends. I chose dark denim with embroidered stars and when Mum finished the skirt and a matching waistcoat, I felt I was the height of fashion.

Mum and I were nearly the same size now, and because she looked so young and dressed in the hippie-like way I enjoyed, I could vary my still-meager wardrobe by borrowing her frilly summer tops. I felt much less dorky now that I wasn't wearing cut-offs. Watching Mum get made up for work in the mornings gave me new ideas about how to be cool. I borrowed her eyeliners and lipsticks and felt more pretty than ugly. A good thing, after years of self-hate.

Mum and I spent a day each weekend cleaning the house and doing the washing. Laundry was still an unwieldy affair in the 1970s, although not as bad as in years past. These were the days of manual twin-tubs: an electric machine on wheels consisting of a top-load laundry tub side-by-side with a spinner. We'd heave it over to the kitchen sink to connect with the hot water tap. Clothes swirled around the tub, but one of us had to remain on hand to fill it with water and keep the other hose hooked over the lip of the sink for water emptying out. Then wet clothes and towels needed to be threaded through a wringer and dropped into the spinner drum. The items, still quite damp, were moved to a basket, more clothes were pushed into the machine, clean water added, and while the new load swirled, one of us dashed into the garden to hang the first set on the line, or else we'd drape them over the clothes-horse hanging from the ceiling over the breakfast area.

In between this delicate dance, there were vegetables to prepare for dinner and vacuuming of carpets. Simon and Wanda played outside, and Dad, if not working, was sent off with a grocery list.

I didn't mind household jobs. It was time spent with Mum, and we swapped anecdotes about school or her workplace, or toiled in a comfortable silence, tongue between lips, concentrating on ironing or rolling pastry.

I enjoyed Sunday night dinners, a time when the five of us sat after the day's chores to eat a roast and joke around. If I cooked a chicken, I always ensured one of the kids found the wishbone on their plate. Little Simon or Wanda closed their eyes and made wishes. After our weekend dinners, I played with them. They especially enjoyed quizzes, when we pretended to be on a TV game show. I asked questions I knew they'd be able to answer if they were learning it in school. I explained to Simon I'd make Wanda's questions easier because she was younger. He got quizzed on such topics as Henry VIII's reign, dinosaurs and famous inventors, and Wanda was asked for the capital city of England, or who was the hairy character in *The Addams Family.*

It seemed weekends were the only time we had a remote chance of all eating together and for me to get to know my new family better. Sunday dinners from these early days in the house are a treasured memory now.

Weekdays usually consisted of just me and the kids eating alone or with Dad, whose conversation was almost nonexistent, while Mum stayed late after work. At this point, I thought she was just extra busy in the office, but I felt her absence and was lonely after the kids went to bed. I'd finish my schoolwork in a mist of depression, sometimes not seeing my mother walk through the door until after eleven at night.

Quiet evenings were difficult. These were the times I thought about Nana, vivid thoughts of her lying stiff underground instead of writing her beloved poems and letters to magazines. Deep in my heart I wanted her back and in the way we used to be years before— cuddling together and playing paper games, or me sitting at her feet while she crocheted cushion covers. I felt adrift and desperately tried to reconcile what had come between us and to feel that she'd loved me. I usually didn't succeed. I continued to see myself as cast out, shoved aside and unwanted, but even if I had been second-class, I still needed her and missed her horribly.

21

At school one day, Colleen walked over. "Hey," she said. "I have news for you. My boyfriend's pal Craig can't stop thinking about you. He wants to give you a ride home on his bike someday."

"Gosh, I wouldn't know what to say to him," I said, flustered. "He'd get bored pretty quickly. I don't have a clue what I'd chat about."

"Oh man," that husky voice exclaimed. "Do you think he expects debates on politics? Just be yourself—after all, I like you as just you! Or ask questions about his motorbike. Guys like talking about stuff like that, you know."

"Umm. I'd better not."

"Look, on the back of his bike, you won't get a chance to talk much anyway. Just enjoy being together. I'm gonna tell him you'll have a ride! Me and Pete'll come too and see you home. It'll be brilliant, man, all four of us bombing through town on the bikes. Besides, you two'll be company for me and Pete."

"Oh, I can't. Besides, what would I wear?"

"You're fine the way you are! Next week then. Tuesday?"

Monday night saw me with another attack of nerves. On Tuesday I arose extra early, ensured my hair was just so and added a hint of blue eye shadow I normally reserved for weekends.

"Why're you so quiet?" asked Babs. "I keep repeating myself. Pay attention, will ya?"

Mandy clicked her fingers in front of me. "Remember us? Let's catch a bit of lunch."

I followed them into the lunchroom and grabbed a portion of mashed potatoes, fish and cabbage. The food tasted okay here, even the beverages didn't. The canteen was something else I'd had to accept, because in Northingthorpe I went home in the middle of the school day to eat. But with the new school miles away from my house, the canteen was my only option.

To this day, though, I have never forgotten the coffee at that school. First, I was not a coffee drinker. I came from a home of tea lovers, but I had no choice. The school lunchroom served coffee and that was that. Second, the coffee smelled and tasted like old ashtrays. Not kidding. Old ashtrays. Once, out of curiosity, I entered the lunchroom early and stood watching the kitchen staff prepare the coffee, while pretending to lean against a wall reading a textbook. I was so sure they threw their fag ends into the brew. They didn't, and I never figured out what made it taste so terrible. Now, I can only conclude the school bought the cheapest dregs of coffee available. As I held my breath and supped at a mug out of sheer thirst, Colleen arrived just as Babs and Mandy headed for dessert.

"I like your lip gloss," said Colleen. "Lookin' forward to your ride?"

I nodded, not telling her I just knew by the time he'd arrived at my street, Craig would be so bored he'd wish he'd never set eyes on me. I was hopeless at school, uncool with the in-crowd and just a total fake. He'd realize he had made a big mistake. He'd tell Pete how pathetic I was. Pete, in turn, would relay Craig's disappointment to Colleen. She'd begin to distance herself from me, and that would be that. I braced myself.

The bell rang, and Colleen and I strolled to the far gate. The two men and their motorcycles sat like Tweedle Dum and Tweedle Dee, with simple expressions of happiness and good will. Pete's BSA had a black tank and shiny chrome. He'd gathered his hair into a neat ponytail. Colleen kissed him, mounted the back seat and held Pete's shoulders, smiling at me. I looked at Craig, who beamed the same cheeky grin I remembered from a few weeks earlier. He noticed my hesitance and dismounted.

"Ever ridden on a bike?" he asked. I shook my head. "Okay," he continued. "You step on this footrest, swing your leg over and find the footrest on the other side. I'll get on, then you can hold onto me for support." He climbed back onto the bike. "Don't worry, this is just a small Fanny Barnett and I won't be going too fast."

I cautiously put my hand on his shoulder. He didn't recoil from my touch or say "Ugh, ugly cow" like the Northingthorpe boys would have and, encouraged, I stepped onto the bike as he instructed. I held my navy school skirt and as modestly as possible swung my leg over and perched on the seat, delicately clutching Craig's other shoulder. We rode through the city, weaving in and out of cars, humming at red lights, droning through greens, nodding and grinning at Pete and Colleen as first they passed us, and later as we passed them.

These were the days before helmets became law. I'll always remember the freedom and wildness of the wind rustling through my hair, the traffic buzz roaring past, and the smells of burning oil and petrol as we swerved around corners and revved to pass trucks and scooters. Craig turned a few times and yelled questions through the noise. "You okay?" and "Like it?" and "Shall I speed up a bit?" to all of which I shouted back "Yes." I needn't have been so concerned about conversation.

The four of us arrived on my street and rolled to a stop at my driveway, the bikes purring like the virile and vibrant machines I now realized them to be. Simon and Wanda and their little friends ran up in awe like I was some cool rock star and gawked in open admiration at my new friends and rumbling bikes. Colleen swung off and walked over.

"Pete and I are going to The Jolly Sailor for a shandy on Saturday night. Maybe you two can come?"

"Great idea," said Craig. "Shall I drop by about seven?" He looked at me, shyly. I nodded, and we all waved before the bikes took off, leaving me warmed and thrilled at the curbside.

"You've got a boyfriend?" Mum gushed, excited.

"Oh, I don't know about that. We're just having a drink with Colleen and Pete. He may not want to see me again."

"Stop being so down on yourself," Mum said. "I'm sure he'll want to see you even more. What are you going to wear?"

"I was thinking the denim skirt and vest you made for me."

"Good idea. Let's go upstairs and see if I've a top you'd like to put on too."

She seemed as excited as me, and we spent a happy hour perusing her tops until I decided upon her white ruffled peasant blouse. She always looked great in it and I hoped I would too.

Craig arrived at seven o'clock on Saturday clad in clean jeans and a black shirt. Mum and Dad came out to admire his motorbike, then waved us off. I was finally on my first proper date and felt admired, pretty and grown up. We arrived at The Jolly Sailor, parked the Francis-Barnett out back and entered via the pub's rear door. The first thing I saw was the replica of a huge seventeenth-century galleon. Coming into the pub from this end, we'd approached the ship front first, and I was awestruck to see a prow and bulkhead bearing a wooden statue almost the same size as me, of a woman reaching with her arm outstretched. We walked past her to a wide gangplank leading through the side.

"Want a drink?" Craig leaned on the bar.

"Lemonade, please." I felt a tap on my shoulder. "Hi, Colleen, Pete, we just got here."

"All aboard, sailor!" Colleen grinned. "Pete, can I have a shandy? We'll find a table."

Sitting by the helm, I took in my surroundings while we waited for the guys. Cannons pointed outwards and a rope ladder dangled from a thick mast. An anchor lay nearby.

The four of us laughed a lot that evening. I finally felt I'd entered the world of adults, even though I was only fifteen. I smiled to myself, remembering my fascination in watching Northingthorpe folks at night walking into the Hare and Hounds, so forbidden to me at age thirteen. Here I was, in a pub that had to be way better, what with a ship and all, and with bikers who were funny and fun.

Craig and Pete saw themselves as greasers but explained the American meaning of the term didn't apply. They were not Hell's

Angels or guys with slicked-back hair. Greasers in England were simply guys with an enthusiasm for motorcycles.

"Hence 'greaser,' which means we keep our bikes well greased." Craig winked.

Pete nodded. "We get so much rain here...if we don't keep 'em oiled, they'd rust in a minute. We try not to get grease on our clothes, though!"

Much of the evening was spent talking about motorbikes and the best areas of the Pennines for speeding around on Sundays, as well as about music and movies.

Hey, Oxford Road cinema's showing Easy Rider next week...I'm apprenticing at an ink manufacturer's now...I like my boss, he's okay...We're going to my brother's place Thursday...I'm gonna buy a poster of David Bowie. And on and on: all cool teenage stuff.

Craig took me home at ten, and I thanked him for a fun night. I was still unsure of myself and wondered if he felt glad the evening was over, so I awkwardly said goodnight and made to walk up my driveway, but he grabbed my arm and gave me a light peck before bashfully gunning his engine and taking off. I figured that little kiss meant he might call after all. He did, two days later, and we began seeing each other regularly. I did indeed have my first boyfriend.

Occasionally now, Colleen joined my little group at school, but more often she disappeared. Independent, she didn't hang out with anyone in particular, and her attention was split between lessons and her radio. She walked me to the bus stop after classes. This was when we hummed to Motown or made weekend plans.

I cherished having company at school and began seeing my new friends on Saturdays too. Babs had us over to dance in her front room. Mandy took me on longer walking trails. Colleen and I sat chatting in cafes or met with Pete and Craig. These young people in their different ways broadened my limited social experiences, and their simple enjoyment of my company improved my severely damaged self-image. I began to feel less horrible and less stupid.

Craig picked me up for motorbike rides in the countryside. Sometimes we'd hang out at his flat watching films, playing music or talking into the night. Around him I felt beautiful. In turn, I thought he was gorgeous. He was also sensible and a great support if I was struggling with school assignments.

School was a struggle. Most lessons were topics not taught at the previous school and went over my head. Knowing about pollination or chemical reactions did me no good here. Instead I suddenly needed to learn about stratified rock for geography and life in coal mines for history, much of this being detail oriented, such as the dates of nineteenth-century factory acts initiated by Lord Shaftsbury. It was a never-ending task to speed-read textbooks to catch up, exacerbated by the fact that I was forced to travel such a distance to school.

The bullies were wearing me down, and I became convinced it was my fault I was picked on. I was too weak, too timid. As well, I felt out-numbered, for they were about ten strong, and I was only one, because although Mandy and Babs and their group were chummy with me, they just ignored Sally's gang and expected me to do the same. The difference was they were not on the receiving end of the slurs, so I had to handle it alone.

To my surprise, however, a few months later Sally, Janet and their gang received a blow to their pumped-up sense of importance. We were in history class when one of the secretaries walked in with a note for our teacher, who read it then said, "I'm to relay this message to you all. It's written by the headmistress on behalf of the art teacher, Miss O'Riley. Here goes: Art is creative expression. Students who wish to be innovative and who have a sincere desire to acquire skills with paints, sculpting and sketching are welcome to continue attending my Wednesday classes. Any pupils who plan to continue the disruption and disrespect that has plagued this course can take notice that as of today, they will not be tolerated in the Art Variety course. At the first sign of any abuse, whether physical or verbal, I shall report immediately to the office and the offending persons shall be permanently removed."

The history teacher folded the letter and looked somewhere over our heads. "I have no doubt at all as to which individuals this letter is aimed at. I will say to those individuals right now, we staff know who you are. You've developed a bad name and unless things change, your end-of-term reports will certainly reflect it. You should begin considering how your attitudes will affect your futures in the real world."

I turned around. On the other side of the classroom, the gang was red-faced and sombre. None of them said a word. In art class from then on, they showed a quiet interest in what Miss O'Riley taught. They seemed unrecognizable to the rest of us, but we were just relieved that, at least on the surface, the nastiness was over.

22

At home, I felt myself marooned on an iceberg. My mother was now assigned as secretary to a man called Andrew and spent more evenings working late. She relied on me to race home from the other side of town to cook for Simon, Wanda, and myself when Dad was on his late shifts. Other times he was home, but may as well not have been.

"Dad, what're you lookin' at out the window?" Simon asked.

"Hmm, the sky, I suppose. Birds going wheee." Dad flapped his arms like a bird.

"The travelling fairground is in town," said Wanda. "Can you take us tomorrow, Dad? Can I go on the rollercoaster?"

"So you wanna go zoom? Zoomy zoom." Dad waved a hand up in a rollercoaster motion. "Time for screams. Hee hee. We can go if you want." He wriggled his eyebrows, grinned and turned back to staring out the window for another hour. Then he snapped out of his reverie. "Dum de dum dum de!" He grabbed one of Simon's toy cars and flew it through the air while saying "brmmm" on his way out of the room.

The kids were too young to see their father's peculiarities. His eccentric conversations were natural to them and excruciating to me. As a self-conscious teenager, I kept my friends, and later my boyfriends, away from Dad, because he'd always embarrass me. All the same, he was good with his children.

Looking back now, I wonder if he had Asperger's syndrome.

On weekends, Mum did stay home, cheerfully for the most part, although her temper still flared. I'd know at a glance what kind of day I could expect, but half the time I never figured out what set her off. Sometimes it was what side of bed she rolled out of.

"Get the fuck outta my way. Wanda, what're these toys doing on the living room floor...how many times do I have to tell you?" Mum opened the window and tossed Wanda's dolls out. "If you don't want them soaked in the rain, get them and take them to your room! Simon, quit making that noise or you'll wish you'd never been born!"

Mum stomped around banging cups on tables and slamming doors. These were not pleasant weekends, consisting as they did of shrieks of frustration and anger, combined with anxious whining and sullen silences from Simon and Wanda, wounded puppy expressions on Dad and increasing surliness on my part.

In many ways, I resembled my mother, not in looks but in temperament. If something went wrong or wasn't to her liking she quickly exploded and stomped around, oblivious to her effect on others. I'm not sure if this is something I inherited or learned from her, but a part of me was the same, if more diluted. I'd put up with almost anything and did indeed endure a lot, to a certain point, after which I'd cross over into fury. The more my mother targeted me in her fits of rage, the more I simmered in silence until she did or said one last thing that sent me over the edge, and then we'd scream at each other like trapped chimps stuck in a small cage.

This was followed by hours or days of not speaking until one of us—usually me—began a neutral conversation about how many loaves of bread to buy or some other mundane thing. The other would respond in kind and so would end our standoff.

Mum eventually admitted to me she was having an affair with her boss, Andrew. She implored me to understand her life, living with someone like my second stepfather. Mum described time spent with Andrew. She attended this or that function with him; they found a new restaurant famous for its T-bone steaks; she accompanied him into an important meeting with regional heads and was asked her opinion; they were planning to go on a business trip together and stay in a romantic hotel.

Mum justified herself by telling me something embarrassing that happened the year before I moved in.

She, Dad and the kids drove south to spend time with my uncle Ed and his family. Ed, still in the RAF, had told his sister about an upcoming military celebration for a senior RAF marshall near his base. A hall was reserved for the black-tie event. Ed and his wife Joan invited my Mum and Dad to join them and, knowing her husband like she did, Mum drilled him on how to behave. No stupid jokes. Try to remain quiet in front of other people, and don't talk unless someone asks you something.

Ed and Joan walked into the banquet hall arm-in-arm, followed by Mum and Dad. They made the rounds, murmuring introductions to various groups before wandering on to greet others. The women were draped in ball gowns. Men wore bowties.

Everyone sat for dinner, the marshall and his party at a long table at the front, surrounded by round tables seating ten diners each. A five-course meal came and went. Mum and Dad chatted to Ed and Joan on one side of them and to another couple on the other. Mum made sure she was sitting directly next to these people to do most of the talking and that Dad was in the middle, where he could sit comfortably quiet, as he preferred. So far so good.

Music began and the marshall and his wife stepped up to dance, followed by everyone else. Ed and Joan began to waltz. Mum and Dad did the same. A few songs in, Joan and Dad joined up, and Mum danced with her brother. They were chatting happily when all of a sudden Ed frowned and stared off to the left.

"What's the matter?" asked Mum.

"It's Ben, sitting back at the table...he's taken his jacket off!"

My mother stared blankly at her husband, who was fanning himself with a napkin. Joan had gone to the powder room.

"Viv, this is a military event. There's a protocol I know you're not aware of, but no man can remove his jacket until the marshall takes off his. It's simply not done. Can you go and explain and ask Ben to put it back on?"

At this point, Joan returned. She and Ed began dancing while Mum moved back to the table to ask Ben to wear the jacket.

"Why?" he asked.

She explained the policy that the men watched for the marshall removing his jacket as a signal they were allowed to do away with theirs.

"Bollocks! I'm hot. I ain't putting it back on," he said. He hated this whole event with its rigmarole and rules, and was in one of his rare bad moods.

"But Ben," she said, "it's a tradition of the military. Men wait until the top man takes off his jacket and then they remove theirs."

"I'm hot now!" replied Dad. "It's bloody scorching, dancing and all. I don't want to wear it. I'll melt."

Mum looked around. She felt eyes on them, even though most people were dancing. Every man except her husband was firmly clad in a jacket. She pleaded with him, but he continued to refuse. She stared at him, panic-stricken.

He sat pouty-mouthed, twitching his eyebrows. "It's rubbish, the rest of us having to wait until some pumped-up twit takes his off. I'm not in the military. I don't have to wait for him." He folded his arms as Ed and Joan returned to the table.

Ed smiled anxiously. "Can you put your jacket on, at least for a little while? I'm sure the marshall will shortly be signaling that we can take them off."

"No," responded Dad, shaking his head from side to side in the manner Mum recognized from similar situations. He'd dug his heels in. "I'm sweating after all that dancing. I'm not going to wear it."

Ed, horrified, glanced up. Everyone at the main table was making small talk now, smiling and nodding with eyes firmly focused on each other, but the marshall had a telltale crease on his brow. Ed knew that he, along with everyone else, was discreetly observing the outcome of this breach of protocol. As the band played on and Ed continued pleading, Mum noticed their table companions had vanished to the other side of the hall. This dreadful faux pas meant they'd keep their distance until the situation was rectified. But it wasn't. Dad finally stood up, complaining about the ridiculous palaver everyone was making, and stormed out.

Mum stared helplessly at Ed, who sat stock-still and pale, knowing he'd be talked about for weeks. Worse, she knew, this could affect his career. She and Joan went through the motions a while longer playing at small talk, nodding, chatting with Ed, who also put on a show for a few more minutes before saying they had better go.

I sat appalled as Mum ended her tale and lit a cigarette. I asked what happened next.

"We found Ben back at the quarters watching television in his pajamas. Ed, as our host, bit his tongue, and I apologized the next day to him for the ruined evening. Ed's a good brother. He knows what Ben is like—*he* ended up sympathizing with *me*, because I was more upset about it than even he was. It goes without saying he won't want us anywhere near his base again though. But, She-she, it's never going to change. Ben is an embarrassment. I can't take him anywhere—I never know what he's going to do. On this occasion perhaps he thought he should be assertive. Well, it's okay to have your own opinions, but he just chooses the wrong times. He can't figure out what's appropriate and when."

Mum stopped and sighed, took a drag from her cigarette and continued.

"Andrew is such a contrast. He's making me realize what I'm missing by being married to Ben. When Andrew and I go out he talks with people and we have all kinds of conversations with folks about world events, or do 'joke nights.' We've made such a lot of friends in our regular haunts. I can be myself and have fun. And he's romantic, She-she, buying champagne and taking me to posh restaurants. I've never had this. I'm mad about him."

*   *   *

"Your mother was having an affair." Dr. Beal put down his pen. "How did you feel?"

"When she told me, I squeezed her arm and nodded my support, even though I suddenly felt like an empty envelope," I replied. "I had no words."

I often found myself staring at a plant in the corner of my shrink's room when something was difficult to discuss. By now I'd memorized every pointy, mint-green leaf and the skinny trunk leaning sideways. Now I studied the glazed pot and decided it was ugly. In my peripheral vision, I saw Dr. Beal sip from his water bottle. Summer was at its zenith and although his office was air-conditioned, the heat burrowed in.

"How did this affect you?" he asked. "You often thought you were in the wrong, yet this..."

"I'd always felt to blame for her messy life," I said. "Mum would never have rushed into first one bad marriage and then another if she hadn't gotten pregnant so early with me. I was glad she felt happy. I knew she'd missed out on all the usual teenage fun because of me."

I hesitated and glanced at him. He waited.

"However," I continued. "I was also confused. What were the ethics of all this? Shit, why was life so complicated?"

"Did you meet this man?"

"Yep," I said. "Yeah, I did."

* * *

"So what's he like, this Andrew?"

This was a couple of days after I'd had a chance to absorb what Mum had told me.

"Visit me in the office next week. You'll be on school break so you could drop by Monday morning to meet him, then you and I can grab a bite."

So it was that I walked into her office building the following Monday, where a receptionist directed me along a hallway to Andrew's office. There sat Mum, looking glamorous, typing at her desk while at the other table a man talked on the phone. He was leaning back in his seat, one leg swung loosely over the chair arm as he wrote notes on a desk calendar. I studied him curiously for a few seconds and he glanced up, smiled easily and waved before starting to write again.

Mum beckoned me to sit, and I stared around the room, thinking about this man and my mother working here week after week, growing closer and fonder of each other. It occurred to me he saw more of her than I did.

"So," he said, returning the phone to its cradle, "you're Viv's daughter. So pleased to meet you. Two whole weeks off school, eh? Lucky you. What are you planning to do? Here, let's show you around." He stood and reached for his jacket. "C'mon, both of you... tour time!"

With that, I was treated to a whirlwind excursion around the building, shown the shop floor, introduced to the sales team and receptionists. Everyone told Mum how lovely her daughter looked, and she chatted happily. I was shy, as I always was with large social groups, but felt acceptance from everyone. I was one of their workers' kids, and as such they'd be kind to me. Andrew suggested the three of us go to the pub.

"It's 12:05. Time to get outta here. Grab your coats, ladies, lunch is on me. Viv, how about the White Hart on the corner?"

Andrew grabbed both our arms so that he was walking with one of us on either side. "How lucky could I get?" he beamed. "Not one, but two lovely ladies today!"

Mum laughed, and I smiled. She was right. This well built, dapper man could not be more different from what she was used to.

Mum now began telling me about her dates with Andrew. I felt split into three during these conversations. One side of me felt needed, for I was Mum's only confidante. Another part of me felt culpable for the kids' unhappiness. They didn't understand why their mother was rarely home. Although I stood in by cooking and playing games, it wasn't the same as spending time with their mother—and at sixteen myself, I was becoming impatient with their needs when my own were so neglected. A third facet was my feeling of being an enabler. Sometimes I couldn't face Dad. He was not a bad man, after all, just a strange one. As the months rolled by, I began resenting Andrew for having more of my mother's attention than we did, and I wondered how his own family was handling the long absences.

Still, I was glad Mum had found happiness, even if only in stolen snatches. When home on weekends, she joked with Dad and me, helped Simon and Wanda with their rehearsals for a school play and took us for fish and chips. Sometimes we'd take off for the amusements and beach in Southport.

During the week when she was absent, the rest of us wilted like flowers in the shade, but when she arrived home with her effervescent nature and warm smile, we perked up like buds in spring. My mother didn't appreciate our need for her, and I'm sure she thought we just went about our day whether she was there or not. She didn't grasp the desire we had to share it all with her—and I think if she ever had known, it wouldn't have changed a thing. She was too in love now, truly in love for the first time, to give Andrew up.

Aged 16

23

"Simon, Wanda, dinner's ready," I called. "Come on while it's still warm."

Mum arrived unexpectedly just as we began to eat.

"Oh, you're home?" Pleasantly surprised, I pointed to the counter. "Grab a plate, there's still stew in the pot."

"The bread's buttered too thickly." Mum's face looked dark as she took a seat. "Why didn't you add more potatoes?" She pushed some beef into her mouth. "Ugh, there's not enough salt in the gravy!"

"Blimey! Maybe you should come home more often and just make it yourself."

She slammed her fork down. "You'd better watch it, I'm warning you," she shouted. "Because I have feelings...and I stopped smoking yesterday, and it's hard, and I'm craving a cigarette, and you're being so mean." She jabbed her finger at me, her eyebrows almost meeting in the middle, her eyes squinting in fury. "You have a nasty streak in you to talk to me like that. Stay away from me."

She disappeared, plate and all, slamming the door to go and eat in the living room. Quietly, the kids grabbed their plates and followed her, anxious to be with their mother under any circumstances.

I climbed upstairs to my bedroom and began sobbing, trying to figure out how to escape. I was increasingly exhausted with wondering what kind of reception I'd get when my mother walked through the door. If she and Andrew were getting along, she was happy and we all relaxed. If she'd had a frustrating week, she was oblivious to what she did to us: words that could not be taken back, expressions of hate impossible to forget, double standards that were grossly unfair.

She'd once complained to me she couldn't take Dad anywhere and that she never knew how weirdly he might behave. It occurred to me now that, like him, she had no self-awareness. I felt the same way about her as she felt about him.

The morning after, I walked to the bus stop without saying goodbye. Mum came home so late for the rest of the week I didn't see her at all until Saturday.

"Hi, She-she." She burst into the kitchen and grabbed a box of cereal.

Her vivacious smile won me over as it always did. She was my mother, after all, and her enthusiastic, girlish grin had always softened me, almost as if I were the adult and she the child. Evidently life was good at the moment. She'd forgotten her insults. I was expected to forget as well.

"I feel like dancing tonight. Wanna come to Alderbarn Hall with me? Super place. Mainly for the over-35s group, but the music's fab. You'll love it, full of tunnels, nooks and crannies."

At the Hall, Elton John's "Crocodile Rock" bounced through the speakers. I twirled and gyrated in my bell-bottom jeans through flashing pink and purple disco neons. I locked eyes with my blonde, blue-eyed mother rocking halfway across the crowded floor in her bright, tight dress, swinging her arms and lip-synching. Surrounded by men, she was soaking up the worship in their eyes. Elton John faded. Now it was Stevie Wonder with "Superstition."

I dipped away from the guys around me and sat at our table, where a drink reached me "compliments of Greg" before I had chance to order cola. "Who's Greg?" I shouted over the noise. The waiter pointed to a clean-cut, tidy man sitting in a backlit alcove by the rear wall. I waved and downed half the liqueur then boogied back to the dance floor. He followed. The three of us—my mother, my admirer and I—bopped to Slade's "Gudbuy T'Jane" and Abba's "Waterloo."

As Mum and I walked off the dance floor, Greg followed. "Can I see you next week?"

I shook my head. "We may be back next month. Let's have a dance then. It's getting late. Bye."

Mum and I exited and headed for the car.

Lying awake after the disco, I thought about how everything had changed this last year since leaving Northingthorpe. Mum treated me as a grown-up, which I liked. I had been thoroughly sick of being treated as a kid and a second-best one at that. Here, living in Mum's house now, our relationship was changing from mother-daughter to confidantes, in between the quarrels. I felt like I counted. She enjoyed taking me dancing with her and asked my opinion when buying clothes. She didn't think I was stupid. We'd become buddies, at least when she wasn't in one of her moods or when I wasn't in deep depression over our loss of Nana.

*   *   *

Dr. Beal nodded. "You once told me you felt your whole life was a series of ups and downs. What you've just told me is a good example: the dinner row followed by dancing. You were shouted at a lot in your younger life."

"And I'd start yelling too. I can be nasty when I'm mad. You haven't seen that side of me."

"And you feel culpable for the arguments?"

"Well, especially with Nana. I wish I hadn't had such rows about Dean. It upset her."

"Sheila, have you ever considered how the treatment meted out to you by others made *you* miserable?"

"Um..."

"No one put themselves in your shoes when you were a child or teenager."

"I didn't put myself in theirs either."

"The difference is, you were five, eight, thirteen years old. They were adults and should have known better or else gotten family counseling."

"God no! In England in those days people would die rather than go to a psychologist. If they did, they'd never admit it. Anyway, how would we pay the fees? With buttons? Remember, we were very poor."

"Regardless, Sheila, you're unfair to yourself. I encourage you be mindful of when you're self-blaming, to ask yourself what others may have done to make you react like you did. We'll continue to work on that."

"Self-blaming...yeah, that's one way to put it." I studied my fingernails and fiddled with my rings. "Y'know, like me, my mother felt disillusioned with life, but unlike me, her depression manifested as shouting and storming around the house. She'd suffered many disappointments and still struggled to figure out what she wanted."

I looked up and Dr. Beal nodded.

"She told me she wanted to enjoy herself, that she'd spent her teens and twenties struggling with money, babies, a horrible marriage, never-ending laundry. She said she was now in a position where she could go for lunch with salesmen who popped in and out of the office, have drinks with Andrew after work, attend social events. She wanted to make up for lost time.

"I was aware that but for me, my mother might have found the man of her dreams instead of two lemons. Who was I to judge if she dated Andrew and had a bit of fun? If she was happy, I was happy for her. But I felt guilty about Dad. I felt like an accomplice in a crime."

"Do you not think, Sheila, that she shouldn't have been telling her teenaged daughter about her affair? It put you in an awkward position, which wasn't your fault."

"That's true. I also felt bad about my ambivalence toward Mum. Yes, her bad start was because of me, but I felt my own miserable life was due to being the defenseless, illegitimate child of a single mother. The kid whose mother had been absent, present, absent, present. Absent at times she was desperately needed. The genuine dislike I sometimes felt for her, coupled with adoration and a craving for her attention, had caused me, in a way, to grow up with a sort of split personality."

"You mean, like two Sheilas inside, battling for control? Is that how you felt?"

"Exactly like that—because my experiences with her weren't all bad. Although I liken those years in my mother's house to being stranded on an ice floe, there were warmer moments. Friday evenings were a favorite. If Mum came home early no other evening of the week, she almost always arrived straight after work on Fridays. This was telly night. After the kids were in bed, she and I would watch *The Twilight Zone* or a Hammer horror film. We loved them and were alternately terrified by vampires in dark castles and amused by campy scenes of Dr. Jekyll diving behind a couch and reappearing in a rubber mask." I laughed at the memory. "I wished she'd come home at a normal time more often, for when we were tranquil around each other, we had pleasant times."

*   *   *

A year after leaving Northingthorpe, Mum and I returned for a visit. I went for a walk with Eleanor and Joss while Dean went to the park with his auntie Viv and Grandad.

It often irritated me to observe my mother with my various little cousins. She was always so charming—blissfully attentive as they sang, and sitting on the floor to play. She hugged them, gazed raptly, infused them with her passion for their games. They lapped it up, and often I wished she were my aunt, too, instead of my mother. Dean was delighted to be going for a walk with her, and I wondered how he'd feel if he had to live with her fulltime. He'd soon find her growing bored with him as her mind wandered back to Andrew. I didn't realize it yet, but her affair was already beginning to drive a wedge between her and me and my half-siblings and Dad.

It seems ironic now, that she allowed yet another office romance to cause repercussions lasting decades. The difference was, older and wiser now, she was careful. And more cynical. She'd recently told me, "Sex is just sex. There's nothing wrong with a fling."

Eleanor wanted to know all about my new life as we walked along Gate Road like we had so many times through the years. I patted Joss and gave her a stick to carry. I missed my dog. I'd been forced to leave her because there was no one in the Manchester house most days to care for her. She was better off here, with Eleanor and Dean at home, and that gave me peace of mind.

"Well, as I wrote in my letter, I even have a boyfriend now, and we go to pubs and cafés with friends. It's so different from here."

Across the road I recognized some guys from the old school, still loitering at the corner of the street and still wearing their bovver boots. When they saw me, they gestured rudely. Instantly I fell into my old, conditioned state of looking down and away, then hated myself for doing so.

"I hike on trails with a couple of school pals, and sometimes I go out with Mum," I continued. "But I'm still not used to Nana being gone."

Eleanor's eyes misted. "I think none of us are," she responded. "Perhaps we never will be."

Dad, the kids and me on a southern beach

24

In the spring, Mandy and I walked through the town center. After searching for weekend work in several shops, we were taken on by a large departmental store. She was in deli and I was on the lower floor in the women's panties section. Some of these were beige. Others were frilly with tie-strings and lace; I fell in love with these and bought a pair. We had a laugh about this at The Jolly Sailor.

"Well," said Mandy, "you should demand more money to model the knickers on the counter top."

Craig laughed. "I'd watch your catwalk. You could sell some to me. Then I'd wrap them and give you as gifts. Provided you model them again at my pad."

"Are they warm?" This was from Pete. "Could I wear them on my head on cold days instead of my balaclava?"

"Be quiet," Colleen giggled. "You want your ears to get cold?"

Before starting my job, Mum decided the five of us should drive to a beach down south for an afternoon, then on to a distant cousin's farm for a few days. I'd never met Harriet or her family.

Dad tramped around the sand with the kids while Mum and I sunbathed. She looked bored. "Right now, Andrew is in Torquay with his family," she said. "It's his birthday. We agreed to think about each other at exactly three o'clock." She closed her eyes wistfully.

I was fed up with hearing about Andrew, but also glad Mum had some joy in her life, so I listened when she felt like talking. "Buy him a souvenir, Mum. A birthday present."

By the time we arrived at the farm, Mum was decidedly irritable but hid it from her cousins. They had one daughter, my age, and I was to sleep on the pullout in her room.

"Lovely to see you." Harriet and her husband greeted us.

"Let me help with the bags." Karl and Ben busied themselves unloading the car.

"Eileen, they're here." Harriet led us into a living room where her daughter was reading a *Jackie* magazine.

Eileen looked at us sullenly. "Hi." She got up and left the room.

Harriet smiled it off. "I made a pie. You must be starving."

We sat around a chunky farmhouse table at the back of a cozy kitchen with terracotta floor tiles and cast iron pans hanging from hooks next to dormer windows. I could hear geese honking somewhere. Simon and Wanda fed morsels to a tan and white terrier. Eileen came in the back door and ate silently while everyone chatted. She didn't acknowledge anyone and left when she'd finished, returning home as I was falling asleep.

As we descended the stairs the following morning, we heard swearing in the kitchen, ending with "friggin' bitch" and a slammed door as she left again. We couldn't pretend we hadn't heard it. Mum asked Harriet what was wrong.

Harriet said her daughter had changed completely since becoming a teenager. Eileen hung around with friends god-knows-where. She scarcely spoke and refused to help around the house or do her schoolwork. "She shouts at me constantly. All I asked her this morning was to pick a few apples whilst I made breakfast. The orchard's over there, it's not even far." Harriet sank to a chair. "I don't know what to do."

Mum suggested she might need to hold her own and make it absolutely clear the behavior was unacceptable.

"Nothing works. I've tried everything." Harriet glanced at me, then asked my mother: "Do you ever have any trouble with Sheila?"

It amazed me throughout my childhood how many people spoke about me in the third-person even when I was sitting right in front of them.

"No, for the most part she's fine. The usual adolescent moodiness sometimes, but Sheila helps with housework and never insults me."

However, Mum's glumness increased as the week went by, and she started sniping at me even in front of Harriet. I stayed out of her way, sitting in the front room playing Eileen's records. On our last morning Mum helped Harriet in the kitchen and I came down late, having slept through two wake-up calls. Mum complained the minute I entered, telling me how lazy I was and how I should be helping with the kids. I told her to back off. I did not need this treatment first thing in the morning. She yelled at me to be quiet. Furiously, I told her to stop talking to me like that.

"Oh, dear," said Harriet. "See, you have problems with your daughter too. I think all teenagers are the same."

Startled, Mum told her I was not usually like this. Harriet just sighed. She picked up some plates and left the room. Mum glared at me.

"I'll never forgive you for this," she seethed through her teeth. "You've made me look a fool. Just when I'd been telling her how easy you were to live with."

"You're the one who started it," I responded. "How come Harriet didn't notice your tone of voice toward me? And she must be mad if she thinks I'm anything like Eileen. I don't swear at you, no matter how shittily you talk to me. But I'm supposed to say nothing when you're accusing me of laziness and all?"

"Shut up! Thank God we're going home. I've had enough of you for quite a while."

The three-hour return journey was strained and silent. She was not the only one glad to get home. I called my friends to meet for a drink the next evening.

I sat in The Jolly Sailor. As I butted out a cigarette I confided in my friends about my home troubles. Colleen suggested I sit my mother down and tell her plainly what effect her actions had.

I shook my head. "She's great when she's in a good mood. Yeah, we can talk at those times, but as soon as something doesn't go her way, she changes. You can't discuss *anything* with her then. But it's me she rants at. Not at Dad, because he doesn't answer back, and she runs out of steam with him. But I'm not made like him. I can't just sit there and let her accuse and shout at me."

"Ignore her," suggested Craig. "The same as your Dad or the kids.

"But the point is I don't see why I should take this crap. I'm not a bad person. She's off gallivanting with that damned Andrew and I'm left to babysit and cook and wash dishes...like an unpaid servant."

"Stick it out til school's over," said Mandy. "Then find a job and move out."

"Seems a long way off," I said. "Y'know, the sad thing is, when she's in a good mood, she's super to be with, like a best pal. I wish she was happier more often."

I sat there pining for the side of her I saw too little of. My friends didn't know what else to say.

*   *   *

At home, the constantly empty house irritated the kids. They were seven and six now, old enough to realize Mum was absent more than their friends' mothers.

Simon took to whining. Wanda asked me for the office phone number. When I said Mum was not at work because it was almost 7:30 p.m., she asked, understandably, "Why isn't Mum at home if the office is closed?"

I bit my lip and shrugged.

"She's never home," she yelled.

I was losing patience with the kids and resented what I saw as their easy life. Their meals were provided; they had no schoolwork or housework, and just played with their friends. I begrudged the fact that their lives were easier than mine. At sixteen I was too young to understand their own unrealized need for their mother was having a bad effect on them. I felt they were ungracious when I was trying so hard to keep the house comfortable. Wanda was mouthy. If I laughed at something on TV, she mimicked me, rolled her eyes and sighed loudly. When I put dinner on the table, she grabbed her plate and headed for the living room. I complained to Mum one weekend, but she shrugged and said girls were more difficult to please than boys.

"Well, maybe you should come home more and deal with it, because I've about had it with her," I said.

Mum did not, however, spend extra time at home, and as the months passed I grew more angry not only with her but with Wanda. This finally got out of hand one evening when Wanda taunted me with "Deaf lugs" on the stairwell. This pushed my hot button. I dashed after her, shoved her into her bedroom and shrieked at her to stop talking to me like shit. She was quite hysterical as I slammed her door and stayed upstairs until Mum arrived.

When my mother heard Wanda's story she began scolding me, and I responded with pure rage until even she backed off. I took to staying at Craig's flat and getting a ride to school, or slept at Mandy's house or on Colleen's couch. I needed companionship, and with Mum's continual absences and moody presences, my boyfriend and friends became my surrogate family.

"Why don't you move in with me?" Craig asked one evening as we sat in a pub near his flat.

I took a swig of my drink. The King's Oak was a traditional English pub full of heavy dark walls hung with watercolors of hunters sitting astride white horses and followed by dozens of hounds. I always detested these pictures, imagining the fox just outside the range of the scene, running for dear life, terrified and exhausted. I reached forward and ran my finger along the wallpaper. It was the kind with a velvety finish in burgundy, the soft texture swirling around a cream, matte backdrop.

I knew Craig was watching me.

I thought about my mother. For the second time in my life, the experience of living with her had proven a nightmare. I realized my life was about to change in many ways, for school would be finished and I could begin making my own choices.

"Let me think about it," I said.

The next few weeks were mostly good with Mum bright and cheerful. She and I went dancing at Alderbarn Hall. We descended on the town fair with Simon and Wanda one Sunday to sit on merry-go-rounds and win stuffed animals.

I felt content at home until Mum asked me where her brown bag was. I said I didn't know and helped her look.

"Isn't it in the wardrobe where you usually store it?" I asked.

"No. Did you borrow it? Is it in your room?"

"I never borrow your brown one. It doesn't match any of my outfits."

"Well, why isn't it where I normally keep it?" She frowned.

"Don't know."

"Fuck!" She began flinging coats out of the hall closet and rummaging behind her hats. "I'm sure you used it last week."

"I did not." Seeing she was becoming aggravated, I scooted downstairs.

After twenty minutes Mum stormed into the living room shouting that her bag was definitely not in the house and that I must have lost it.

"I never used your damn bag!" I slammed my book on the couch. She banged around the house yanking things out of cupboards, all the time blaming me for something I'd never touched, then flung open the front door and went to have coffee at her friend Vera's house, leaving the kids staring at me. I could see what they were thinking: *Mum's left the house again and it's your fault.*

I climbed the stairs slowly and lay on the bed. My life was pathetic—I was pathetic. The world was a dark ocean of disillusionment. I was tired, so tired. How could I end it all? This thought had crossed my mind occasionally. I pondered it once more, discarding the idea of hanging myself in case I botched it and ended up with a broken neck and paralyzed for life. Slashing my wrists wouldn't work if someone found me bleeding and rushed me to the hospital for stitches, and then I might have paralyzed hands. I'd thought of these possibilities and knew I didn't want to be alive and handicapped and unable to try again.

Suddenly, an idea hit me and I sat up, gaping at the light fixture above. Electrocution would be instantaneous. Standing on the bed,

I removed the shade and unscrewed the light bulb, then walked to the wall and turned the switch. The connection was now live. All it would take was for me to push a couple of fingers into the opening. I stood awhile, staring at the dangling light socket. The room faded. Background noise from downstairs dwindled and my surroundings became misty. The only clear object was that light socket, its grey pleated wire flowing from the white ceiling, the round, black socket just a few feet away.

I was numb, except for a dark mass in my chest as I thought of Nana, how she shoved me aside, how I became unimportant to her. How I was irrelevant to Grandad, to my mother, to everyone. It was better this way then. Maybe I'd meet Nana in the next life and we could start again, somehow. This world, here, was simply not working for me.

It dawned on me that I hadn't cried much when she died, just once when Antony talked to me that morning way back, and another time at her funeral. Why hadn't I cried more, I wondered, as I climbed up, keeping my balance. I stood, hesitating, gazing at the black opening of the socket just above me, inside which I could see two metal prongs I knew were just itching for a connection. I studied them, still wavering, until I heard the front door slam. My mother had returned. Quickly I grabbed the socket and pushed in my fingers. A strong, sharp jolt flung me to the floor where I lay, my body quivering uncontrollably for a minute before I recovered, realizing with disappointment that I was still here. I could hear my mother telling the kids to get ready for dinner, so I quickly turned the switch off and replaced the bulb. I lay back on the bed with the palms of my hands covering my eyes, shutting out the world.

Half-an-hour later, Mum called up that dinner was ready. I stayed where I was but then she called my name, so I went down and ate quietly. She was now in a good mood, but I let the kids chat to her. I didn't want to. Then I caught sight of her brown handbag on the kitchen counter and stopped eating. She saw me looking and said cheerfully, "I forgot—I lent it to Vera. She just gave it back."

The next morning, after everyone left the house, I phoned Craig.

"Come and get me."

Craig arrived in his new three-wheeler car and soon I was settled into "our pad." For the second time in my life, I got away before being fully destroyed. When it dawned on my mother I'd left, she phoned Craig to see where I was, and I told her I'd return only to collect some stuff and that would be it.

Things were changing in other ways too. Colleen and Pete split up and Colleen found work in Somerset. I missed her terribly. We exchanged letters for a while, but it petered out. Mandy entered the military. She was posted to a base in the south of England, assigned as a driver, eventually obtaining a license to drive buses, trucks and ambulances. I was happy for her and we still keep in touch.

Eventually, my mother invited Craig and me for dinner and made an effort to get along. There was peace between us once again.

Aged 20

25

I lived with Craig for two years. We had good times, but we were young and finally outgrew each other. We departed on good terms and kept in touch for a while.

One day I saw a nanny job advertised in a travel magazine, and by age nineteen I was teaching English to kids in Spain. Thus began more than a decade of working abroad, with occasional returns to Britain to stay with my mother for as long as I could stand it. Living with her for short periods worked out better, and when she became too much I'd simply take off for another few months abroad. I worked as a waitress, barmaid, English teacher, farmhand and shop assistant, in Germany, Greece, Israel and Belgium. I finally had fun.

By age twenty-one, my curiosity about my other half-siblings, Jeanette and Dana, got the better of me. What were they like; what kind of lives were they living; did they know about me? Back in England in between jobs, I went to find them, looking up the street name Mum once mentioned. I recognized their home as soon as I saw it: the hell house of my childhood. Sitting on my motorbike for half an hour, I stared at the house and garden, remembering the beatings, the cupboard-prison, the window I jumped from. My terror of the "sausage" and the slipper. I sat immobilized, frozen.

A young woman emerged from the back door and threw a bag into the metal dustbin near the fence. It was probably the same one in which Terry had burned my drawings all those years ago. She started back to the house, but then turned to look at me and walked toward the fence. I made to switch on the ignition, but changed my mind and instead watched her approach. She asked if I was lost. I hesitated before I spoke because I was so taken aback at how much she resembled our mother.

"Is it really you?" she asked. "Sheila? My older sister?"

When Jeanette realized who I was, she wanted to know all about Mum, me and any other sisters or brothers. She urged me to come in. I balked, but she pleaded and finally—impulsively—I decided I should. After all, what could her monstrous father do to me now? I was old enough to defend myself, but I knew it wouldn't be necessary. Terry would behave all sweetie-pie in the presence of others; he always had. It dawned on me that Jeanette had no idea of what he put me through and I was not about to tell her.

I locked my bike, clenched my teeth and marched through the front door, wondering how I'd feel. As I stepped into the hall, I eyed the living room entrance. I couldn't see *him* yet, but I heard the television and saw the back of a tartan armchair in the same spot in which he had always sat.

I felt strangely weightless and glanced at the floor in front of the window. This was where Terry bent me over and caused blood to flow down my legs, and suddenly I was there as that four-year-old child, screaming in pain and fear. Just as quickly, I was back in my own body, standing tall, my hands clenched. *He cannot hurt me anymore.* I heard Jeanette saying, "Guess who's here." I walked in defiantly as he turned.

He didn't know me until Jeanette explained, then his face froze as I marched to the middle of the room. I stood straight, eyes unblinking, and took in his surprisingly small frame as he sat there, peering from behind the thick black glasses. His hunched-over position was so horribly familiar—the way he crouched with his knees together and his feet sticking outwards like some sort of anemic bedbug. That this scrawny, sickly-looking creature, whose hair was crying out for a good wash, had been capable of such horror, that he had changed me from a cheerful, curious, happy-go-lucky youngster into a shattered, fearful little girl whose childhood became a permanent wreck, made me want to scream.

I couldn't speak. Half of me wanted to claw him, punch him, shut him into the cupboard where he'd locked me. The other half was battling the instinct to cringe and crawl away, and I remained stuck in a silent tug-of-war.

Jeanette chattered on about fetching tea and dashed into the kitchen, leaving us alone. Still he did not say anything as he gazed at me from his chair. Slowly and deliberately I sat on the scruffy sofa I used to sit on. I found myself inspecting him as I might a half-rotted amphibian in permafrost.

A memory oozed into my mind: the way I had always sat statue-still in this very spot, trying to be invisible as Terry watched TV, bent forward and peering through his thick lenses after spending his daily hour of amusement with me. He looked at me now through the squinting eyes I remembered so well, and then he faltered and tried to make small talk. It petered out when he received no response. The air between us was thick. I was battling so many urges: to shriek at him for stealing my life; to run out of that house of horrors and keep on running; to storm into the kitchen and tell Jeanette the truth about her father.

I did none of these things. First, recalling his sadistic glee in watching my four-year-old face when he forced me to witness my pictures burning made me realize the satisfaction he'd get in knowing his impact hadn't ended after I left. Secondly, I determined then and there I'd inform Jeanette of his deeds when the time was right.

Revulsion and loathing and nausea rose in my throat. I concentrated in controlling myself for the sake of my half-sister.

Jeanette returned with tea that he drank and I didn't, then another girl walked into the house with a smile that turned into a frown when Jeanette introduced me.

"Don't mind meeting you, but I do not wish to see our mother," Dana said.

"Why?"

"She left us."

"Do you know she tried to get custody of you?"

"She went off with our Dad's best friend. And never came back to see us. Not in all these years."

"That's not quite..."

"Don't want to hear it. Sorry, I'm leaving. Bye."

Dana walked out. I never happened to see her again, but understood her resentment. After all, she'd never heard Mum's side of the story: Mum's attempt at getting housing for her girls, her lost fight for custody, the negative picture painted by their father and the young girls' increasing consternation each time their mother visited—how Mum finally gave up for everyone's mental health. I thought if I eventually told Jeanette all these things, she'd tell Dana, who then would come around, but it never happened. However, I knew where Dana was coming from, for I had also experienced the hurt of abandonment. It was what I'd felt when my beloved Nana began doting on Dean, no longer needing me.

Jeanette took away the cups, and Bluebeard continued to watch me silently, his claws grasping the chair arms. I got up. I didn't want to stay in this house for another minute, and I called to Jeanette that I was leaving. Her father carried on sitting where he was. He shook slightly and suddenly I knew he was afraid. I glared at him, sickened by the enormity of his effect on my life, and then walked out followed by Jeanette who asked for our mother's phone number. I told her I'd better warn Mum first and promised to contact her soon and bring her to meet our mother.

Back home I spent the evening lying on my bed facing the ceiling, my eyes unseeing as I relived the day's events. It dawned on me that I hadn't known what to anticipate when I sat astride my motorcycle, facing the house. At most I thought I might glimpse one of the girls, but I had not anticipated interaction. I'd merely wanted to see them, but the day had unpackaged itself in an entirely unexpected direction.

I wondered if I was supposed to feel differently now that I'd confronted my demon, but this wasn't the case. It was not a cathartic experience but simply a realization that the monster was still just that. The pedophile that terrorized me seemed gigantic to the tiny girl I'd been, and although to my adult eyes he now appeared small and weak, his monstrosity remained enormous. What he'd inflicted created terror that remained for years; my resulting timidity and feeling of worthlessness caused me to be bullied relentlessly by children in my school. They took my apprehension to be weakness and stupidity, and my resulting poor schoolwork and social behavior were further consequences of the ripple effect of the terrible year in his hands.

I slept restlessly, dreaming of hyenas laughing hysterically in shadowy caves, and awoke early to lie for hours, remembering my miserable youth, the feelings of betrayal and abandonment by my grandparents, of being told by Terry that Nana hated me, of being beaten and locked in a cupboard, of the lack of my mother's empathy during that year, all welling up in turn. I felt resentment toward them all. Everything had contributed toward what that little girl had become: a loser, a scaredy-cat, a dunce.

Then I recalled my re-entrance into the house the day before. It dawned on me I hadn't been afraid anymore. I was ready to defend myself and fight if I'd had to. I'd stared *him* down; *he* had blinked. I'd now traveled, seen the world and survived it, surmounted the meanness of schoolkids, the second-hand treatment, the moods of my mother. I realized I was able to walk away, fearlessly take off and live in other places, experience adventure, explore new lands— enjoy myself. I had learned to continue on regardless.

The following morning, I perched on my mother's bed as she readied herself for work. She sat on her stool facing the dressing-table mirror, applying cream to her cheeks. The back of her head was toward me, curlers hugging her hair.

"Remember the street you told me you lived on when you were married before—on the other side of Manchester?" I said.

"Oh yes, why?"

"I found it. Drove there yesterday."

I couldn't see Mum's expression as she began screwing the lid onto her jar of cream.

"It's exactly as I remember from all those years ago. The whole street is the same," I continued. "I met Jeanette. I met Dana too."

My mother dropped her cosmetics and swung toward me, falling to her knees and burying her head in my lap. She screamed in grief and I stopped, shocked into silence as she clutched my legs and continued to weep while kneeling on the floor. Dad hurried in and we looked at each other, startled.

"What are they like?" She searched my face whilst tears streamed down hers. "What are they like? Tell me, tell me..." And she collapsed into uncontrollable sobs.

*   *   *

Dr. Beal seemed pleased about my long-ago self-assessment after this unexpected encounter. He asked me how I felt about my mother's reaction.

"Surprised. That's all. She'd hardly ever talked about them, at least not to me. I had no idea what she felt."

"And you?" he asked. "You say there was no sense of catharsis from the visit. But I believe there was. Think of how you faced him—that must have given you strength."

"Not really." I shrugged. "I hadn't even begun to heal. Still haven't. Why d'you think I'm here?"

"Because of what he inflicted, certainly, but also because of *all* the other letdowns and abuses. Sheila, I have a plan for how we're going to go forward, something I think will work for you. We'll talk more about it in a couple of weeks."

*   *   *

Mum and Jeanette had a private reunion shortly before I left for a six-month job in Wales. I returned to discover my belongings packed into boxes and Jeanette ensconced in my bedroom, with Mum's explanation that Jeanette had wanted to get to know her other family. Mum explained that because I liked to travel, I wouldn't need the bedroom much and she suggested I sleep on the living room couch.

Trying to be understanding, I agreed, only to discover the lack of privacy as well as the inability to sleep until everyone had gone upstairs was more nerve-wracking than I expected.

Jeanette was like our mother both in personality and looks: bubbly and attractive. With Mum absent so often, I was glad of a sister my age to hang around with. I invited Jeanette on evenings out with my friends and when we were alone together we talked about our childhoods, lives lived before we knew each other.

"I've often wondered," she began one afternoon, "why things didn't work out between my parents."

I hesitated then spoke, my voice almost a whisper. "I have to tell you something. Your father treated me really badly. He beat me, screamed at me and…and…" I breathed in. "Your father sexually abused me. This is part of why Mum eventually left him."

"What do you mean?" She gaped at me. "How?"

"He…" I suddenly found it impossible to talk in detail, although I'd wanted to bring it up for so long. "He, um, touched me. And made me touch him. Wank him off. Many times." There, I'd said it. But I couldn't say any more; this was already too difficult. I found myself sweating.

Jeanette looked at the floor and then slowly up again. Her mouth was tight.

"I believe you," she said. "He touched me sometimes too."

I gasped. "But you're his own daughter!"

She nodded. "I know. But when I was younger he'd make me stand there and he'd touch me. Just sometimes." She shrugged, embarrassed.

I was shocked, although I suddenly realized I was not surprised. "Did he hit you as well?"

"No, he was always nice to me, other than those times…"

"What about Dana?" I asked. "Did he do that to her too?"

"I doubt it," she said. "He treated her with kid gloves. She was his favorite. Maybe cuz she looks like him, or cuz she's the youngest. He always treated her as the baby of the family, even though there's only two years between us."

"I see." I recalled the favoritism my grandparents had directed toward Dean. "Did that make you hate her?"

She shook her head. "Dana and I are pretty close. But I never told her about this. I sometimes wondered if he touched me because he missed my mother. But now you're telling me he did this to you all those years ago…so it wasn't just me."

"Oh, it definitely wasn't just you. He obviously likes little girls!" I found myself gripping the cushion I was leaning on. "You should tell Mum. She's known what he did to me for quite a while. Maybe now she'll report him. It's not just my word anymore; we're both witnesses."

A week later, Jeanette informed me that she had indeed told our mother. "She was really angry for me," Jeanette nodded. "She's going to report it to the authorities."

But, as the months wore on, it appeared to be forgotten. I eventually asked Jeanette if Mum had done anything. She told me she was still waiting.

I figured nothing would happen. Mum was too busy being out and enjoying herself with Andrew. Jeanette and I never raised it again, although I did consider going to the police myself, on both our behalves.

However, this being the late 1970s, when these assaults were still hushed up or not believed, I realized the odds of getting anything done by anyone was rather hopeless. Perhaps Mum felt the same way, although I wished she'd talked to us about it. It is only relatively recently, decades after the fact, that victims of Jimmy Savile, Rolf Harris, Larry Nassar and others have come forward, some of whom tried to complain as children or teenagers and were not believed.

26

I continued to cook and clean. I believe this was my attempt to hold the family together in a real home. Nonetheless, I began to resent being taken for granted. No one else took the initiative.

As an experiment one evening after catching a bus home from a movie with Jeanette, I suggested a late-night supper, something I often rustled up when any of us came in after a night out.

"How about cheese on toast?"

"Sounds good," said Jeanette.

"Okay. Can you make it for a change, while I get my nightshirt on?"

"What? Oh, I dunno, I'm tired. Let's forget it."

I knew that as soon as she realized I wasn't intending to make it as usual, this would be her response. It annoyed me. "You liked the idea of supper a minute ago."

"I don't wanna cook at this hour," she complained.

"You're always happy enough to eat as long as I'm the one fixing it! Look, Jeanette, I think you need to start helping out more around the house. It's always left to me. I get tired sometimes."

"Fine, if you're so insistent about food, I'll make you some." Jeanette walked ahead quickly and opened the front door. She threw her coat onto the bannister and stormed into the kitchen.

Sulkily, she turned the grill on. We ended the night arguing. From then on her humorous outer layer was brushed aside to reveal the fangs and claws that lay behind it.

Other things upset me too. Whenever my handsome new boyfriend came over, Jeanette piled on make-up and dressed provocatively. She was someone who wore tee-shirts around the house, so seeing her suddenly dash to the door when she knew my date was arriving, flinging it open with a flourish, hand-on-hip and wearing skin-tight dresses, was something I found shocking. I didn't even need a "woman's intuition" to realize what she was trying to do; it would have been obvious to anyone.

One evening my boyfriend and I decided to stay in and watch TV. Jeanette waited for the commercials and got out of her seat, pretended to yawn whilst stretching her arms up and simultaneously thrusting her breasts forward. She proceeded to strut over to the television, bent over more than necessary to turn the volume down, then turned to look my date coyly in the eye before wriggling back to her chair. I finally told my mother, who confronted her and reported back that Jeanette sheepishly admitted being flirty, saying it was harmless but she'd stop if I was so insecure. *The bitchy little tramp*, I thought. I'd never have done this to someone.

I needed to get away from this house before I became depressed again. Besides, I was tired of feeling like an outcast. I'd had enough of the couch and lack of privacy. My boyfriend moved abroad to work and it was time for me to venture out too. I'd become good at doing this. Since jumping out of the window at age four, albeit unsuccessfully back then, my philosophy had been, "If an out-of-control bus is bearing down on you, step out of the way."

I called my old school friend Mandy, now living in York. "Come to my place," she said. We shared her rented house in the countryside and I worked in a shop. Mandy, with her placid nature, shone sunbeams that soothed me, although I did still see my mother from time to time when she and Andrew traveled through on business. They'd meet us for a pub meal and she was at her best: happy, jocular, laid-back. Andrew batted off jokes like tennis balls.

After two years of rural peace with my friend, I was ready for city life again and returned to my mother's home, hoping things would be better. I made an effort to reacquaint with Jeanette and put her previous disloyalty behind me, but Wanda began picking arguments once more, always backed up by Jeanette. Mum was still mostly absent, much to my disappointment, for it was her company, as well as a sense of belonging, that I craved. Things hadn't changed. I began to visit friends, spending less time in the house and less time cooking and picking up after everyone. One afternoon I sat quietly reading until my mother and Jeanette barged into the living room like charging buffalo and demanded to know why I wasn't pulling my weight around the house.

"Let's see," I said, counting on my fingers. "Until recently, I spent two hours every Saturday grocery shopping in Tesco's, queuing at the butcher's, bringing all the bags back and unloading them...every single weekend. I cooked meals for everyone day in and day out. If Dad's not working, he cooks, too, but who else does? Sundays, I'm often left to do laundry on my own for six of us. And although you do your own ironing, when do any of you iron my stuff? After all, if I'm laundering, cleaning, shopping and cooking, I don't really have much time left if I'm supposed to have a life."

"Well, you always seem happy to volunteer," Mum responded. "Anyway, I help out when I'm here."

They both leaned against the wall side-by-side as I continued.

"What do you do around here, Jeanette? I can't think of a single thing other than you occasionally vacuum, which takes all of twenty minutes. And you, Mum, it's your house. You ask Simon to clean the car for pocket money. Ditto for Wanda, who washes the Sunday pots for pocket money too. Where's my reward? How much should I charge? You and I used to do housework together. It was a joint project. Now you're either out with Jeanette or the kids or at a neighbour's or with Andrew. Or with me...yes, you and I still get together sometimes...after I've done the chores."

Red-faced, both of them left the room.

I continued to enjoy my time with my friends. The matter wasn't raised again, the house became messier, dinner was now a random occurrence with everyone heating soup for themselves when they were hungry, which they did anyway when I was working abroad. I grilled myself bacon butties and ate in front of the TV, having given up on joint dinners at the table. I wondered if I was being egocentric and childish, but if I was, so what? Everyone in this house was

was egocentric and childish. Mum began cooking again when she was home, and I let her do it by herself.

I continued in a detached but friendly fashion as much as possible, and sometimes still went to see a movie with Mum. Occasionally, I invited her and Jeanette for a drink with my friends at The Old Oak, a new pub in the town center. However, my new *laissez-faire* approach was difficult for them, and at home they'd sullenly ask me to help out. I would, provided I saw them also working. But I despaired of this so-called family ever becoming a real one.

Then came the straw that broke the camel's back and made me leave for good.

One evening, Mum dressed in a skirt and blouse she'd borrowed from me. I asked where she was going and if I could come. She answered no. She and Andrew were taking her friend Vera out for her birthday. She couldn't change the reservation now so maybe I could come another time.

The following week I came in from a hike and found Mum and Jeanette laughing in the kitchen.

"Hi," I said as I pulled off my boots.

"Hey, let me show you my new photos," said Jeanette. As she made to pull the packet from her purse, my mother caught her arm and shook her head. Jeanette smiled and shrugged.

I was puzzled by the exchange. "What's wrong?"

"Oh, nothing," Mum said, looking startled as Jeanette handed the pictures to me one by one.

It was the final photograph that made me stop and stare. There, beaming at the camera, were Mum and Andrew, with Mum's friend Vera—and Jeanette. I recognized Mum's outfit as the new clothes she'd borrowed from me that evening I'd asked if I could come. I realized, from this photo, she'd invited Jeanette for the birthday dinner but not me.

Slowly I looked at my mother. She was wearing an expression not dissimilar to a petty thief caught stealing on camera. I was scarcely able to believe this proof of her deceit—and she looked at me, embarrassed and silent as I stared at her. Suddenly, she jumped up, eyes blazing, and yelled, "What, for Christ's sake, is the matter now? Fuck, I can never do anything right; quit moping!" She stormed out of the kitchen, slamming the door.

Speechless, I turned to gaze at Jeanette, my mask of nonchalance completely smashed. Narrowing her eyes, she sneered, grabbed the picture, walked slowly to the door and, turning to me one more time, smirked and left the room.

My mother never approached to explain; instead, in her customary manner she stomped around for weeks, expecting me to forget and make up as usual. Anytime I entered a room, she and a very smug Jeanette would silently walk out of it and slam the door. My mother's inability to admit her mistakes and apologize had gone too far, as had her betrayal and duplicity. She'd made it glaringly obvious she preferred Jeanette's witty companionship, and her subsequent cavalier attitude gave the malicious Jeanette a knife with which to exacerbate my wound. I'd had it. I moved into an apartment.

As the months wore on, I wondered if my mother would at least try to repair the breach before December; after all, Christmas was family time. However, as the weeks passed, there was nothing but silence. I was in disbelief. My mother was accustomed to me making the first move after arguments, but in this case, I was just too disappointed and hurt to do this. It was her responsibility to rectify this treatment, but as Christmas approached I wondered if she really cared.

She knew where I was for I'd asked Dad to help me move, but there came a time I realized I was waiting in vain for her knock. The second-class treatment I'd endured at age ten from my grandmother had now been repeated tenfold by my mother.

It was left to my trusty friend Mandy to pick me up on her way to spend Christmas with her parents in Blackpool. By now she was completely disgusted with my mother's consistently childish behavior, as she put it, and she told me to stay away from that house for my own good. Mandy helped me a lot, as did other friends, but what none of them could do was reconstruct my shattered life. I changed. And I stayed changed. A ball of rage grew in my chest and it remained.

In the spring, I left England again and traveled for several years, living and working in various countries, meeting new friends, dating, drinking and dancing with abandon. I clambered towers of medieval churches, took photos of ancient ruins, sunbathed on crisp, white sands and climbed steep, rocky hills, keeping myself as busy as possible and refusing to think about Manchester or anyone in it, although there were bad days when all I could do was lie in bed. Those were the times I wondered what was so awful about me that people, strangers and family alike, found it so easy to treat me like shit. There had to be something lacking in me: personality, behavior, intellect. Something made me insignificant, like a runt animal. But that ball of fury kept me going. The hell with them all, I thought. The hell with them!

This sense of self as useless made me refuse to become attached to anyone. I wouldn't let people close enough to see the real me, the stupid me. Instead I became the party girl: joking, laughing, letting guys drive me to expensive mountain restaurants in Athens, arranging disco nights with the girls in Tel Aviv, joining friends for a weekend expedition to Amsterdam. I had fun, new adventures, exotic meals. Two gal pals and I spent one Christmas Day ambling around the Parthenon and posing with a Greek Santa; four of us floated in Israel's Dead Sea and covered ourselves with the famous mud; a boyfriend took me to Bruges and we ate French fries covered with sesame mayonnaise.

I took advantage of my youth and energy and ensured every waking minute was filled. I wrote to my aunt Eleanor with news of my adventures and mailed postcards to Grandad and my uncles, but I never sent a letter to the house in Manchester.

Finally, I returned to England in 1984 and stayed again with Mandy, occasionally visiting Eleanor and other relatives. I didn't feel like telling them what had transpired in Manchester. I simply told them I did not want contact with my mother and that I didn't want to talk about her either. By now Mandy had moved into a small flat closer to York. I worked part-time and went to college.

Perhaps it was being back near the seat of my pain, or maybe it was the fact that I was aware of my mother's strong presence just a couple of hundred miles away, but I began again to slide into depression. The treatment I'd received from her now hit me like a ton of bricks; I'd escaped my memories and feelings whilst out of the country, but now recollections of her and Andrew visiting me in York, our laughs and fun then replaced with arguments back in Manchester, and her final, obvious preference for Jeanette began weighing on me.

I'd never asked my mother to choose between Jeanette and me. I'd hoped family was family regardless of the shortcomings all humans have. But my mother had chosen nonetheless, and the image of that merry picture of her, Andrew and Jeanette with Vera, me excluded, scorched my mind in relived scenarios all over again.

I didn't consider ending it all this time in the way I'd tried in my mid-teens. I was too angry now. My attitude was more "fuck you all" than "sorry I'm a nuisance." The popularity I'd experienced during my travels and the many friends I'd made and admirers I'd acquired made me realize I was as good as anyone. I had a right to be here.

Instead, in summer of 1985 I decided to leave Britain for good. Being so close to the seats of my rebuff, Northingthorpe and Manchester, was not good for my well-being and I realized I had a more carefree life when I was away, far away.

Mandy drove me to the airport and waved me off. I landed in Canada and have made this my home ever since. Apart from rare, brief visits, I haven't returned to England and I don't miss it very much, if at all. I yearn for the history: York Minster, Stonehenge, Britain's 11th-century pubs and Roman ruins. Nothing else. There is nothing else at all.

But this is still not the end...not quite. Those rare, brief visits became defining moments.

27

Dr. Beal opened his door, stepped into the lobby and nodded.

"Come in, Sheila." His face quickly fell as he saw my expression, but he just as speedily resumed a soothing smile.

Flopping into my usual chair, one of four placed across from him, I stared at the plant.

"How are you?" I mumbled. "How's your father-in-law?"

"My wife is with him," he replied. "We're told it won't be much longer. I'll need to answer my cellphone if it buzzes. Hope you don't mind. My daughter's on her way home, too."

"I totally understand." I looked at him. "If you have to dash home, it's okay."

"Thanks. It likely won't come to that, not today." He settled into his listening pose: head tilted, legs crossed, pen poised. "How have you been? It's two weeks since we talked. I suspect you've been ruminating on the events you recounted last time, am I right?"

"Yeah." I turned my gaze back to the spiky leaves. "My mother preferred her other kids...I know it's me. I'm the idiot nobody wanted."

"No, you're not."

"You're paid to say that," I snapped.

"Sheila, remember my saying I have a plan for how we're going forward? We begin now." Dr. Beal leaned forward. "A psycho-analysis of your mother."

"What?" I turned toward him. "But she's dead."

"You've relayed enough details that we can come up with reasons for her behavior."

Baffled, I waited for him to continue. Suddenly the memory of a book I read five years earlier seeped into my brain: Sigmund Freud's *Leonardo Da Vinci and a Memory of His Childhood.* I mentioned it. "In the same way Freud used Vasari's first-hand accounts from those who knew Da Vinci, you can figure out possibilities for my mother, is this what you mean? What her triggers were, her reactions and so on."

"Exactly," he said, pleased with my comprehension.

Curious, I nodded for him to continue.

"I'll explain bipolar disorder."

"Oh, I don't think..."

"Not bipolar I. I want to discuss bipolar II."

"Oh, right. There are two bipolars. What's the difference?"

"A lot," replied Dr. Beal. "Less-intense elevated moods in bipolar II. Hypomanic episodes or hypomania. There's also hyperthymia. Our understanding about these is still evolving. And something we call rapid cycling." He waited for these bewildering terms to sink in.

I stretched my legs and crossed my ankles, settling my spine against the back of the chair. "I'm listening."

"Bipolar II's mood swings are less intense. People experiencing hypomanic episodes, for example, are very pleasant when they're "up": the life of the party, jocular, a passionate interest in people and activities. Contagiously positive. The euphoria can last some weeks, followed by depression and erratic actions, low energy, feelings of guilt and worthlessness."

"The description's rather general. I used to go to pubs where everyone told jokes and were pleasant. And if people are miserable about something, sure, they'd be low energy."

"We're just exploring ideas for now. Symptoms of hypomania include extremely attractive personality traits such as charisma, high self-esteem, energy, not needing much sleep, flying from one idea to the next, sexual vitality, creativity and an outgoing personality when on a high. This doesn't sound so awful, but at the other end of the spectrum are impatience, risk-taking such as overspending, selfishness, arrogance, bad temper, boredom and indifference."

"Hmm, some of those do sound like her," I said. "It's true my mother had these affairs. She sure had a sexual and energetic vitality, and guys were always looking at her. She was the life of the party when in a good mood. But lack of sleep? That's not her. She liked her sleep in between late nights out, often dozing while watching TV. No overspending. Her good moods wouldn't last some weeks either. They'd last a day or several, and then something would upset her. External thing, not something internal."

Dr. Beal nodded as he wrote notes. "I want you to understand these terms, but it'll take time to narrow the possibilities. I'll describe hyperthymia..."

"Isn't that when someone dies of cold?"

"No, that's hypothermia." He smiled. "Hyperthymic temperament is like hypomania but less so. So again, extroversion, joviality, expansiveness, self-assurance, low threshold for boredom and so on. Excessively positive spells. But the moods are more stable than hypomania."

Dr. Beal spent the hour explaining various traits and answering my questions. I wanted to know where I could read more. He suggested I come in whenever I wanted, to sit in the lobby and read his *DSM IV* manual. It was the go-to book for mental health professionals. I spent the next two weeks poring over the syndromes he'd described. I also read up on PTSD and related subjects. They were a fascinating read. I realized how much better we could understand others and ourselves, just by being aware of external psychological triggers and innate or copied responses.

By coincidence, I then heard about hypomania on TV.

It was now 2011 and Maria Shriver filed for divorce after discovering an affair between her husband, Arnold Schwarzenegger, and their live-in housekeeper. A Canadian TV journalist interviewed Dr. John D. Gartner from the Johns Hopkins University Medical School. He is the author of *The Hypomanic Edge* and *In Search of Bill Clinton*. The journalist was trying to get a feel for the kind of individuals that take such risks, willing to sacrifice everything for a brief moment of satisfaction. What makes people like Schwarzenegger and

Clinton tick? What gives them the confidence—many would say the stupidity—to act in ways that, if caught, would lead to humiliation and loss? Dr. Gartner discussed the traits of hypomanic temperament, and I pricked up my ears. It was as if he, like Dr. Beal, was describing my mother.

I found Gartner's *In Search of Bill Clinton* and read it in a week. Although I cannot compare my mother's intellect to that of the former president, there are many folks with hypomanic or hyperthymic temperaments who also never made it to the White House. But creative? energetic? impulsive? I was able to put a check mark next to so many traits I was stunned.

Gartner researched the past life of the former president via interviews with those who knew his family. His chapters on Virginia, Clinton's mother, made me realize a person's exceptionality didn't have to be absolute in order to fit the description of hypomanic personality. What Gartner discovered about Virginia proves an ordinary but high-energy individual can fit the profile: high self-esteem, hedonism, exuberance, outbursts, extroversion. Perhaps finally, decades after the many hurts she'd inflicted, I was about to acquire some understanding of my own mother's behavior? Maybe her bad choices in life were not just because she'd had me so early?

I recalled that during my teen years Mum had house decorating fits every few months. I might go hiking on a Sunday morning and return home mid-afternoon to find the furniture repositioned. Every couple of years, she'd repaint one of the rooms, add new wallpaper, throw out old bedspreads. She did a lot of this herself in a robust frenzy while everyone kept out of her way. She also maintained a fulltime job and, back then, regular household and gardening chores. She took acting courses and went to modeling school, thinking she'd be in demand with photographers. I remember watching in a hall in Manchester's city center as my mother learned to walk on a model's runway.

Mum was most definitely charismatic. It was how she became so successful in her office job in the 1970s, moving from secretarial to management and eventually into sales. She loved being around people and got on especially well with men. And eventually the energy she directed toward house and family came to be redirected toward Andrew.

*   *   *

In our next session, I told Dr. Beal that although many traits fit my mother, hyperthymia and so on couldn't be what she had. Her moods didn't switch gradually over several weeks but rather over days or even hours.

"Yes, and now I want to talk to you about a mood disorder that is irregular and unpredictable: cyclothymia. It creates chaos for the person affected and for those around them. Rapid cycling is disruptive because no one knows what to expect from one day to the next. Changes are frequent..."

"But here's the thing." I stopped him. "Even if my mother had any or all of these things, and it's possible she did, it doesn't address the fact that I was always the one who got the worst of it. Not the others. She'd shout at them, but she didn't pull on them what she pulled on me." I folded my arms. "Y'know, she could have been a vampire for all I cared, turning at every full moon. It's the fact that I got the brunt of it...why me? None of this analysis answers that."

"Actually, it might. Just bear with me."

Inwardly I sighed. I was becoming mixed up in all these names, but I nodded. Dr. Beal continued. He repeated back some of the incidents I'd described in past months, which demonstrated Mum's love of dancing and excitement, the socializing, her energetic bursts of activity. And her boredom with routine, needy kids, her bouts of irritation and unreachability. I waited until he'd finished.

"But regardless, I'm the one she kicked in the teeth."

"I don't believe she loved you less than her other children."

I folded my arms and looked out of the window. "You're wrong. What she did..." I stopped, unable to voice it any longer.

"Sheila, you told me that when she had outbursts, her other kids, her husband Ben, her siblings, they all just stayed quiet until the wind finally went out of her sails. Then everyone carried on as normal. Right?"

"Uh-huh."

"But you didn't. You couldn't. You'd had enough abuse through the years, at school, on the street, wherever. You only tolerated her insults and accusations for so long, and then you'd push back, many times as loudly as she did. She was accustomed to everyone letting her get her way, and when you didn't it further triggered her outbursts and she became worse. Had anyone else put their foot down like you did, they'd have received the same malicious treatment."

I let this sink in, saying nothing.

"I truly believe your mother loved you as much as her other children. Think how happy she was when you wanted to leave Northingthorpe and move in with her. Think about how she wanted you back when you were four. But whichever condition she had— likely one of these I've been discussing—you pushed her hot buttons. It wasn't your fault—you had a right to defend yourself— but it fanned the fire. In everything you've told me, I've seen this pattern. Her screaming fits, everyone going quiet, her returning to normal. Her screaming fits, you shouting back, her anger reaching fever pitch. No matter what she hurt you with, if you were the type to shrink away she'd have calmed down and expected everything to return to normal no matter how much she'd demeaned you. Remember the traits I explained...at the negative end: indifference, arrogance, erratic actions."

*   *   *

I read Gartner's *The Hypomanic Edge*. Not everything in his books described my mother, but there were hundreds of adjectives and phrases in what I read that kept me returning to the same answer: my mother had likely had some form of this temperament and this is what made her act like she did. Time and again throughout my young years, and in my twenties when I finally left home and her, for good, I'd blamed myself, believing I was nerdy, stupid, and that's why she treated me the way she did. But was so much of it really my fault? Perhaps not.

I began to wonder if my mother inherited her angry outbursts from Grandad, who'd mellowed by the time I arrived on the scene, but who, my uncles and aunt told me, was extremely strict when they were kids and yelled loudly at them for the slightest perceived naughtiness. As small children, they trod on eggshells for fear of offending their father.

Dr. Beal, I thought. *You may be right.*

28

The first of very few trips back to Britain happened four years after immigrating. It was 1989, the same year the Berlin Wall was torn down. I flew over because my aunt had been ill. I stayed with Eleanor and her family in Sheffield and then went to Mandy's in York. Eleanor tried to talk me into attending Ed's wedding. My uncle was getting married for the second time. By huge coincidence the event was to be in York right when I'd be staying with Mandy. I declined, explaining I didn't want to see either my mother or Jeanette. Nothing my aunt said changed my mind. Eleanor described my mother's troubles in the last few years; it turned out she and Andrew, now living together, had made bad investments.

"It will cheer her up to see you," said Eleanor. "And there'll be a lovely reception."

"No," I said. "Besides, Ed didn't send me an invitation."

"Sheila!" said Eleanor. "He didn't know you'd happen to be in the country. You've been away so long. You know Ed would love you to come. I'll tell him you're back."

"Definitely not. Anyway, it's better this way; it'd be pretty icy with me and my mother and Jeanette in the same room. I wouldn't want any awkwardness to spoil Ed's day."

"Sheila, please..."

"No!"

After a few days in Sheffield, where Eleanor continued to try to change my mind, I went on to see Mandy. She'd bought a charming little home near a village of granite houses and was excited to show me her surroundings. Her puppy dug holes in the garden and two cats wandered serenely in and out of the back door. Mandy was ever drawn to the quiet life. Staying with her in the scenic locations she chose had always been akin to entering an oasis.

I wanted news about her parents in Blackpool and told her about my travels. We drove into York, bought fish and chips on the way back, and after dinner I mentioned the fluke of my uncle's wedding happening in York in two days. Like my aunt, she tried to persuade me to go. Again I refused.

"Sheila, it'd be a chance for you to see everyone—"

"I will not be in the same room as my mother and Jeanette. Why would I put myself through that again? Have my mother behave as if I don't exist and have Jeanette smirking at me?"

"Your mum won't do that, not after having written that letter."

Mandy was referring to an unexpected letter my mother sent to me in Greece a few years earlier after getting my address from Eleanor. The envelope had contained old photos, a card, and a handwritten note telling me she missed me and the laughs we'd often had. She'd said it was soon going to be her 50th birthday and how it would be the greatest thing if she got a letter from me. I never responded.

"No, Mandy," I said. "After the way she treated me? She went too far. You know that."

"But if you attended the wedding you could sit with your aunt or grandfather. Let your mother and Jeanette see how well you are. You know what they say: living well is the best revenge. Honestly, you look so fit, make 'em jealous."

She tried coaxing me some more until I finally said, quietly, "Mandy…I just can't."

She sighed, then changed tactics. "Okay, here's what you do. Call your mother and tell her you're here in York and that you'll see her if she wishes. She can come here. Have some private time together. I can go out." She proffered the phone.

"Are you out of your mind? You *know* how she treated me." I walked over to the window and stared at distant fields.

Mandy continued sitting next to the phone. "Look," she began, "you're in the process of getting your papers…you'll be a Canadian citizen living thousands of miles away."

I stayed silent.

"You won't come back to England much, if at all…this is a golden chance to listen to what she might have to say. Maybe you two could at least make peace."

All I could remember was being screamed at, lied to, used and abused. I sat and folded my arms. "Why would I want see her?"

"Sheila, think about this. You've moved to Canada. Years will go by and your mother will age and eventually die. Or maybe she'll be in a traffic accident a year from now…who knows…but this may be the only chance to ever see her again. How would you feel if she got killed in a crash next year?"

We stared silently at each other for a few minutes.

"Sheila, you two had good times once. You did get along at least half the time. Think of how the two of you used to laugh and joke when she came to York with Andrew."

I shrugged. Any good times were cancelled out by her treatment of me later on as far as I was concerned. I understood what my friend was saying, though. I might never again have a chance to hear what my mother would have to say, if she had anything to say. Mandy offered me the phone again. "C'mon, Sheila. Just do it."

I grabbed the receiver and called Eleanor, asked her for the number, then dialed it. I recognized my mother's voice on the answering machine and left a curt message.

It rang half a minute later and Mandy handed it to me.

"Hello, She-she." My mother was sobbing. "Yes, I definitely want to see you."

Mandy arranged to pick me up in an hour, then drove away, leaving me at the country pub. I saw my mother watching me from a quiet lounge off to the side, cheeks as pale as clouds. I could tell she was nervous. I was not. I was simply on the slow burn I'd felt the last nine years.

"Hi," was all I said, sitting down. I shrugged, a way of telling her to go ahead, speak. Explain.

Her hands shook—a lot—and she reached for her soda as she attempted small talk, asking me how I liked Canada, how long was I staying at Mandy's. I responded briefly, making no attempt to converse. I had a gigantic concrete question mark stuck to the crown of my head. I wanted an answer, and she knew it. And she was hedging, trying not to cry.

So I asked some questions back: What are you and Andrew doing now? Where are you living? How are Simon and Wanda? And finally, why didn't you want me to come when you took Vera out for her birthday? Why did you invite Jeanette and exclude me? Why treat me second-class? Why lie about it all?

My mother offered some lame response about how Jeanette had learned of the outing and begged to tag along. So my mother asked Andrew, who was paying for the dinner, and he'd agreed, but reluctantly, because he had a lot of expenses during that time. She felt she couldn't ask him again on my behalf, and so told me they'd already made a reservation just for herself, Andrew and Vera and couldn't change it because the restaurant was full to capacity.

This explanation didn't make sense. She could have put something toward the bill. Even asking me to contribute would have been better than what she did and how she behaved afterwards. I said as much. I told her that her subsequent treatment of me was unforgivable: refusing to speak or even attempt to make up before Christmas. It was only thanks to Mandy's family I hadn't spent Christmas alone that year.

At this point Mandy walked in and my mother stood up, despondent. "A whole hour gone already?" She smiled half-heartedly at Mandy, who promptly invited her home for a pot of tea before I had chance to say no. Mum brightened and followed us in her car.

The three of us sat on the sofa. It was easier with Mandy present for we were able to chat about impartial things such as the dog. I brought out photos of Canada, making sure my mother knew I never intended to live in England again. Mum bit her lip and nodded.

Finally, it was time for her to leave. Just like everyone else, Mum tried to encourage me to go to Ed's wedding, but I didn't change my mind on this. As much as it would be nice to see Ed, I simply refused to be anywhere near Jeanette, whom I regarded as Lucifer personified. What my mother had done was bad enough, but her other daughter's smug malevolence was something I would never tolerate again.

Mum asked if she and I could at least begin writing letters once more. I nodded. She left and two days later unexpectedly appeared at the airport to see me off. I hadn't mentioned when my flight was, so I don't know how she found out.

This was the start of a slight thaw in our cold war, and although I couldn't bury my resentment, we began to write occasionally. I received newsy, many-paged affairs and wrote some back. She invited me for Christmas. I declined, but when she asked again the following year I slept under her roof for the first time in over a decade. It was a semi-detached red-brick with a tile fireplace and thick grass in the garden. I found a writing desk in the living room I hadn't seen since I'd left Manchester years earlier. Memories of using it for schoolwork flooded back.

Andrew cooked the traditional dinner, and on Boxing Day, Simon and Wanda showed up with their spouses. My mother knew better than to invite Jeanette. I felt neutral toward my half-siblings and had no urge to stay in touch. After all, neither of them had ever tried to contact me. But I put on a show of being pleased to see them for my mother's sake, and we had a pleasant visit.

29

Mandy's words were prophetic, because a year later I received a note from my mother to say she'd been diagnosed with cancer. She was starting chemotherapy and there was a good chance of recovery. I decided to visit in the spring and phoned to tell her. Andrew told me she was out, so I devised a plan with him whereby he'd come to the airport without telling her.

"You can pretend you're shopping," I said. "Pick me up and just leave the car in the driveway with me inside. You go in and act normal. I then knock on the door. You let her answer, and I'll be standing there. It'll be a complete surprise."

Andrew chuckled. "Great idea."

And that is what we did. When I knocked, I braced myself for what my mother might look like. Andrew told me she'd lost her hair. When she yanked the door open she was wearing a headscarf and sweats, her eyes widening as it dawned on her who it was. "Hi," I said, grinning. "Just dropped in from Canada for a cuppa."

She gasped, backed away and sat on the bottom stair, her hands on her cheeks, speechless. Andrew and I laughed and I stepped inside.

"She-she," she said. "Oh, She-she!" It was several minutes before she could speak again.

I stayed with them for two weeks. Mum looked unexpectedly well, with color in her cheeks and just one bout of chemo to go. Even without hair she was striking; she'd never lost her wide smile. Her blue eyes were as breathtaking as ever.

I cooked healthy lunches. I bought comedy videos and we laughed hard at *Trains, Planes and Automobiles*, and *Beetlejuice*.

The three of us walked in the park and visited neighbours. We stayed close to home. I preferred to just see Mum and Andrew and pass on family visits. "Let's just have quiet time together," I'd suggested. We read health magazines. I recommended protein drinks. It was during this visit that Andrew raised the issue of our split-up again, and we found ourselves discussing the night the two of them had treated Vera to a birthday dinner and taken Jeanette.

"It was a spur of the moment thing," explained Andrew. "Viv mentioned her friend was turning forty and I suggested we take her out."

"Yeah, so?"

"So we hadn't originally intended to invite anyone else. It was to be just me and your mum and her friend…"

"That doesn't really take away the fact I was lied to, does it?" The old resentments rose again.

"Well, I think because suddenly I was asked if Jeanette could come, your mum felt that…"

"Listen, both of you," I said. "Maybe Jeanette asked before I did. Fine. But when I asked to come, I was told a lie and excluded. And it wasn't only that event, Mum, it's been the way you treated me my whole life. You were always shouting at me, blaming me for something. And even though you didn't know everything Terry was doing to me way back, you still let him scream at me."

Andrew looked at my mother. "Say something," he said. "We all need to talk about this."

My mother remained silent.

I felt the need to pour out my feelings. "You told me I couldn't come, gave me an excuse even though Jeanette was invited, and you even asked to borrow my new outfit for the event! You always put me on the back burner…"

"I thought it was harmless, just a night out, you could have come another time."

"It's not the point. I don't buy this crap about there not being enough room at the table, or that it was too expensive to have five of us instead of four. You let your other daughter go and not me. I didn't ask you to choose between her and me, but that's what you did. And when I found out—because Jeanette made sure I found out—you gave her a thousand knives to stick in the wound by yelling at me and then ignoring me ever afterwards. She loved that. Why did you do it? What is so irritating, or boring, or awful about me?"

"Sheila, I shouldn't have done it. I've found out a lot about Jeanette since then. I've learned she has a very nasty streak. She's evil in many ways."

Andrew nodded. "Yes," he said. "Hard as nails and sly as hell. We could tell you a lot."

"You made your choice." I shrugged. "You get what you ask for. But I grew up feeling worthless and you helped me stay feeling worthless."

My mother stared at the ceiling and Andrew said nothing. We both waited for her to speak, but when she did it was to change the subject.

"Tell me," she asked. "I've lost so much confidence in the last ten years. I think it's because the business failed. How can I get myself back to normal?"

My mother had not changed in one thing: she could never bear being wrong.

I let it go. What was the point? Anyway, my mother was recovering from a major illness and I didn't want to continue this conversation. It would hurt her as much as it was hurting me. We began talking of other things, and that afternoon she and I walked to the shops. I treated her to an ice cream and we sat on a park bench watching the birds.

"Do you remember me whistling in Grandad's garden and all the sparrows flocking for food?" I asked.

She nodded. We both smiled.

And a few days later, back at the airport, I turned to my mother.

"You come visit me, next time," I said. "In Canada, after you're better. I'll show you around."

She gave me that wide smile and nodded enthusiastically. "Definitely," she said.

30

Although given the all-clear, my mother died three months later. I caught the first plane, my ribs feeling like splintered glass, and arrived the next morning. Andrew again picked me up. What a different experience from when we both drove home from the airport the last time.

After dropping my bag off, Andrew and I went to the funeral parlor. There she lay, her hair having finally grown in a little, grey now but fuzzy like a baby's. She was thin.

It turned out she hadn't been able to keep food down recently, even though the treatments were finished. But that's not what killed her. It was what Andrew described as a pinhole, an opening no one knew about. It allowed a leak of fluid from her chest cavity into her lungs. She'd felt very ill two days previously and was in the hospital for observation.

A nurse called Andrew around 5:30 a.m. to tell him she was gone.

She'd had trouble sleeping and at dawn asked the night nurses to help her to a chair near the window. She'd said, "I'd like to watch the sun rise." Mum had collapsed on the chair while gazing out the window.

* * *

"You know," Dr. Beal said as he shifted in his chair. "Since coming here, you've talked a lot about missing your Nana and needing to talk to her. Many times you have repeated the wish that she'd materialize so you could spend time together. I haven't heard you express that need to see your mother. Why do you think this is?"

I thought for a while. After relaying this last scene I'd stayed quiet, allowing my mind to empty out.

"That's true," I said, finally. "It doesn't mean I didn't grieve for years after Mum'd gone. But...I guess, I had that last visit and did raise the hurts she'd inflicted. Even though we didn't quite resolve it due to the stupid excuses n'all, the fact that I was able to tell her my side was enough. That, and the fact she admitted to missing me terribly after I walked out and that she'd seen the nasty side of Jeanette. Both she and Andrew said that. I felt vindicated. And in the end I was able to put it aside and have peace with her. We left on a good note."

Dr. Beal scribbled. I sighed and waited for him to finish.

"It was different with Nana," I said. "I never got a chance to sort things out with her." I stared at him with beseeching eyes as tears drenched my cheeks for the umpteenth time. "It's why I need her so badly. I can't bear it. I feel so horrible about the arguments we all had when I was a teenager in that house. But please, you have to think of my side of it too. I was sidelined all the time, at school, at home, I was yelled at or ignored and I was going through hell. It was hell."

"Sheila, I believe part of it is also because, from being very young, your grandmother was your substitute mother. With the exception of the year in Manchester at age four, you were raised by your nana. She was your mother figure from the time your mum left you with her when you were a year old. And you have idealized her. To you she was perfect in the way only young children see their parents. You blame yourself, because you think she could do no wrong..."

"She *was* perfect," I said. "Her legs had given out, yet she hobbled around using furniture for support. She never complained about it—always so stoic. All of us idolized her, not just me. She was special. She made clothes, baked, wrote stories...always busy... taught me how to make pastry, write poems, play board games."

"She did wonderful things, certainly." Dr. Beal nodded. "However, she had flaws just as all humans do. In her later years when you all argued in that cramped janitors' house, don't forget how your needs were not met. You were a young teen suffering more than the usual teenaged angst, and nobody, including her, really bothered to make time for you."

"You didn't meet her. She was a caring person. All her children loved her. I shouldn't have been so much trouble. I think she gave up on me. She got really angry sometimes in that last couple of years, even with Grandad and Eleanor, but mostly with me. She swore a lot in her bad moods, which she'd never ever done before."

Dr. Beal slapped his hand to his forehead. "*She* was depressed!"

I fell silent, astonished.

"That was it. She was in discomfort, sick, trapped in a tiny house, affected by not only your problems but also her own. Her daughter was a divorced single parent, her husband's financial situation was always a struggle and it all finally got to her."

I closed my eyes, realization flooding my very pores.

"It was not all your fault, Sheila."

His words were rosebuds blossoming into a soothing shade of soft pink.

Slowly I nodded. Very sad now, but somehow relieved, I nodded.

* * *

Mum was bubbly and loved having people over. As well as our relatives, many others attended her funeral. But someone called Andrew the night before, chatted with him and then he handed the phone to me. He looked strained. I asked who it was. He told me: "It's your mum's friend Vera." Here was the woman they'd taken on that birthday outing.

"Hello, Sheila," she said. "I'm sorry about your mother."

"Oh, right, thanks."

"I won't be there tomorrow," she continued. "I thought about it, and I simply can't. I don't like funerals. I know you'll understand. We'll all miss Vivian..."

"Yes, she'll be missed," I said, and without another word I handed the phone back to Andrew. The irony of this person being the object of the split between Mum and me, her knowing my mother for decades and then not paying her respects, was too much. I didn't want to listen to her for a moment longer.

Andrew and I collected the urn the morning after the cremation. It was Andrew's idea that we scatter the ashes over the cliffs of a seaside village in Wales they'd often spent time in. "It's a lovely place," he said. "I'm sure you'll agree when you see it."

There is nothing so awful as picking up a small box and knowing your parent is inside it. As I held it I found it surprisingly heavy, and the thoughts of my blue-eyed, pretty mother being reduced to the size of a small square was like nothing I'd ever experienced. It is beyond description. I imagined her holding me as a baby. I was now holding her.

Somehow I made myself imagine her in the box, small and vulnerable, with her spirit close by, watching the scene. *We'll do good by you, Mum*, I said in my mind. *Let me cuddle you, Mum*. And I gently drew the box to my cheek, closing my eyes and gently rocking her. "I'm right here," I whispered. "And so's Andrew."

Andrew was right. She is now in a special place, high on a cliff overlooking the sea. We spent an hour climbing, carefully carrying her and stopping to rest every so often. The whole way to Wales, I sat in the passenger seat embracing the container close to my heart. I know l loved my mother, despite everything, and I was not going to allow her to be on the back seat. She was in the front with us. We were travelling as a threesome.

When I returned to Canada, it was with an old box of her things… which then remained unopened for many years. I hid the box in a cupboard and hid my pent-up feelings in my heart, not allowing myself to deal with them.

* * *

Okay, so where does this leave me today?

When I finally opened that dusty old box, memories flooded back of my teenaged angst: my resentment of cousin Dean, my fury at Nana, my huge rows with Eleanor. I realized all this caused Nana great misery in her last years. How could I bear it? I suddenly wanted her back, and very badly. I needed to talk to her, desperately, and although I'd hardly cried at all when she'd died—just once the day of her death and once at her funeral—now, more than forty years later, at home alone whilst my husband was at work, I began to sob, and that turned into a storm, an unleashing of grief I'd pent up for most of my life. I cried and cried, found myself screaming her name in the frantic way I'd called for her from that upstairs window all those years ago when locked in the bedroom by Terry.

I cried, too, with the realization that this time, there could be no train ride to reach her. And I felt I couldn't stand it. This is when, in 2010, I knew I needed professional help.

Dr. Beal imparted invaluable guidance after he heard my story and witnessed my despair. An important turning point in our sessions came halfway through our year together. I'd just read out to him yet another letter from the old box and was alternately filled with anguish, guilt and anger. He gave me a parable based on a recent case. A couple and their 16-year-old were seeing him. The parents were troubled by the boy's rebelliousness, tardiness and apathy. Dr. Beal listened awhile, then asked the boy for his story, insisting each party hear and repeat back what the other was saying. After this exercise, he asked the mother how she felt. In an outburst she said she sometimes hated her son. She said this in front of the boy. So what Dr. Beal did through ensuing visits was get these individuals to deconstruct their negative feelings into parts: anger, hatred, guilt, impatience and so on. He explained to them that their hatred, for example, was not directed at the other person, it was directed toward the *behavior* of the person.

Something clicked. This made sense. On subsequent visits, I let Dr. Beal guide me through each of my feelings separately. He explained I'd likely always grieve at the loss of my grandmother and always despise some of the actions of my mother, but that we could alleviate it. We worked to unbraid my emotions. I realized that what I thought was a general hatred toward a lot of things, was actually not that at all; it was a mixture of negative feelings that resulted in my misunderstanding my own mental reactions. To isolate and analyze each emotion was hugely helpful. I was breaking up a jigsaw puzzle of cuts and bruises.

A big one for me was guilt: feeling everything was my fault. Dr. Beal made me realize I was a child back then. A kid who, by mid-teens, had lost the only family I knew at age four, been taken to a strange new place where I was beaten, sexually abused and emotionally scarred, then finally returned to my grandparents only to be further traumatized by bullying at school. Then I was misunderstood at home. In between it all was my trepidation over what mood my mother would be in on her visits. There was my move to her home after Nana's death and the new family dynamic. All this by age fifteen. Dr. Beal explained that my behavior was a consequence of the many issues I'd undergone. It was understandable. My own misdemeanors were often reactions against the treatment being meted out to me.

My year in psychotherapy helped clear much of the substantial guilt I'd carried. It is really not a cliché to state that a huge weight has been lifted from my shoulders. I'm just a normal person, no better…and no worse…than anyone else. The grief, too, has eased, although I still dearly wish Nana and Mum could materialize even for an hour to talk to me.

As for anger, well, most of the time I'm fine. There are still days when something triggers me, reminds me, and I'm instantly transported somewhere back in time. On such days, I'm best left alone. I can usually sleep it off after a day or so. But I did reach the point where I didn't want to carry the past into the future any longer, and now my bad days are considerably fewer. I don't have flashbacks anywhere near as much as I used to.

Thanks to help from Dr. Beal, even without complete resolutions to the events in my life, I continue to survive, realizing not every story has a proper ending. That's life. Real life, not nice movies or storybooks. No guarantees. I got no apologies from anyone, but I can live with that, finally. After all, I'm not perfect either. I hurt some people too, and now they're not available for me to say sorry to. It's the way it goes. We must get up, learn from it and try to do better next time.

Living previously on the road in Europe with a backpack, picking up jobs where I found them, was therapeutic and life-transforming, but not far enough away from the hurt. Canada was farther but that could assist only so much. I was forced to acknowledge to myself that dealing with bad memories means doing just that—dealing with them. I know there will always be an unhealed part of my heart. However, the wound is smaller and I'm thankful.

And as well as professional help, the patience and love given to me by my beloved husband over the years has gone a long way toward bringing me back to life. I've made good friends and have a happy home. At last I belong in the world.

Funny...I visited a fortune teller once who told me the second half of my life was going to be much happier than the first. She was surprised, saying it's usually the other way around. But she was right.

Epilogue

I am sitting in my study. In front of me is the large, opened box of my mother's things, the one I'd brought back after her funeral in the mid-90s. As you now know, it remained closed for years. It might still have been untouched but for my uncle Bobby's passing away in 2010 after a short illness just a few months before he and his wife were to revisit us. Oh, Bobby. So easygoing, you were...so full of life and down-to-earth. So kind to me. I remember again the bike rides: young Bobby pedaling hard uphill, three-year-old me perched on his handlebars and merrily telling him to go faster.

My aunt Eleanor sent a picture later that year of her with Antony and Ed—each of them standing white-haired and slightly stooped. I stared at the picture a long time, painfully aware of two empty spaces where Bobby and my mother should have stood.

The loss of Bobby plus Eleanor's photo caused me to recall so many things that I'd decided to open the musty old container. Slowly over some months I began pulling out items one by one. It wasn't easy. It was like yanking seven-headed, writhing gargoyles from Pandora's Box, then discovering they could not be caught, could no longer be shoved under lock and key. However, there was something in me needing to do it. I needed to confront these demons. Canada had not been far enough away, and things had been tapping under this lid for quite a while.

Today, several years after first opening it, I peek again into the box. What might I come across this time? I have only been able to do this a little at a time, this encountering of years-old, small items holding such gigantic meaning and up-to-the-minute associations. Today I pull out a beautiful sepia photo of Nana sitting on a swing

My grandmother at three years of age

when she was about three. There is no leg caliper, so she hadn't yet been stricken with polio.

And what's this? A birthday card. My green-crayon handwriting telling Mummy to have a wonderful day is clumsy and misspelled, so I must have been about six. Nana would have enclosed my little card with a letter to her daughter, and Grandad or Eleanor and I would have walked to the phone box near the park to wait for the assigned time of my mother's call. We'd stand inside the red telephone box and tell her our news, and she'd tell us hers and promise to come visit soon.

I realize now, thanks to Dr. Beal, that my mother was merely human and had her own problems. She did the best she could between her missteps and I remember that once she loved me enough to keep me, way back, even in the face of the mid-50s shame and gossip she knew she'd endure. She had parents who supported her and all their children unconditionally, poor though they were. She and I were lucky to have them.

A couple of years ago I had an epiphany about my uncle Antony's dislike of me. I was describing a childhood event to my husband and had just finished telling him again about the special relationship I'd once had with Nana.

"She and I did everything together when I was small. All her kids were older, you see, and I guess I came along at the right time, when she wasn't feeling as relevant in her children's lives. She doted on me. I made her feel needed again, at least until Eleanor's son Dean arrived. I just wasn't accustomed to occupying second place after being so essential to her. After all, I was not that significant to anyone else. I needed so much to feel I was important, at least to her. I was still only ten myself and wasn't used to a new baby taking the stage..."

I suddenly stopped and wondered: was that what had happened to Antony? He was ten also, when I appeared on the scene. Had he been bumped from being the baby of the family, just as I had? Was this why he'd despised me so? I recalled my fury at Eleanor's son and it occurred to me that ten-year-old Antony must have felt like me when his accustomed place in the family vanished. He'd have had to put his needs on hold while Nana was tending to me, in the same way I'd been forced to step aside for Dean. Perhaps he felt pushed out, misunderstood, forgotten—just like me.

"It wasn't my fault, Antony," I muttered to myself. And it dawned on me in the same instant that it wasn't Dean's fault either.

I realize now, with Nana being a middle daughter herself, she had only a limited idea of the special needs of an only child, especially one who'd experienced abandonment, abduction and abuse by age four. Those first formative years cannot be erased, and my resulting behavior was hard for others to comprehend. My uncles and aunt had no knowledge of what childhood could be like for an isolated little girl with no brothers or sisters with whom to play, share baths and stand in solidarity. I was caught between being too young for my teenaged uncles and aunt and too old for the half-siblings and cousins that arrived more than a decade after my birth. I also have half-siblings I've never met: my father's children whom I tried to meet, once, and who had no desire for contact. And here's a marvelous fact…I no longer care. Not at all. What is past is past. And what will be will be.

I'm about to close this box now, after these forages of the last few years. Everything I'd pulled out is back inside, except the little rag dolls Nana made. I framed them recently and hung them on a wall in my bedroom. I gaze at them often now, with warmth.

I'll store the old box in a cupboard and perhaps revisit it again one day. But nothing in it will haunt me next time. I know this for sure—I'm home free.

About the Author

Sheila E. Tucker is a writer, poet, graphic designer and painter. Her work has been published in numerous anthologies, magazines and newspapers, garnering critical acclaim, including one of her poems selected for inclusion in McGraw-Hill Ryerson Canadian school reading lists, and an essay published by the University of Toronto Press.

Sheila recently served as editor-in-chief for an Ontario anthology of prose, visual art and poetry, and she founded and hosts Poetry&Prose, a monthly literary salon in Oakville. She studied English literature at the University of Toronto, is a member of The Ontario Poetry Society and the Heliconian Club for Women in the Arts and Letters, where she is active in selection committees, book projects and author events.

Born in northern England, Sheila moved to Canada in 1985 and eventually settled in Toronto, where she worked for eighteen years as a professional editor and graphic designer. Prior to that, she travelled extensively, working as a private English teacher in Greece, a nanny in Belgium, a barmaid at a Spanish resort, a donut baker at a Welsh holiday camp, kitchen help in an Israeli kibbutz, farmhand in an English quail farm and a boutique manager in British Columbia. Her many adventures included climbing Masada to meditate on the Roman siege, dodging bullets during the Iranian Revolution and scaring off flashers in Waterloo, Belgium. She intends to write a book about working with people!

Sheila currently lives in Oakville, Ontario, with her husband, David, a professor, TV producer and author.

Nana's rag dolls